CONFESSIONS

of a

Working Girl

a true story

Miss S

Published by Sourcebooks, Inc.
P.O. Box 4410, Naperville, Illinois 60567-4410
(630) 961-3900
Fax: (630) 961-2168
www.sourcebooks.com

Originally published in the United Kingdom in 2007 by Penguin Books.

Library of Congress Cataloging-in-Publication Data

S, Miss
    Confessions of a working girl : a true story / Miss S.
        p. cm.
    "Originally published in the United Kingdom in 2007 by Penguin Books."
    1. S, Miss. 2. Prostitutes--Great Britain--Biography. I. Title.
    HQ185.S15 2008
    306.74'2092--dc22
    [B]
                            2008025809

Printed and bound in the United States of America
POD 10 9 8 7 6 5 4 3

To everyone that's paid a price.

Monday 29th September 1997: The First Shift

Evening shift 6 p.m.–1 a.m.
3 x normal service = £60*
2 x £5 tips = £10
Total earned: £70
Clients to date: 3

*M*r. Tights Man wanted to see me and I hadn't even said hello. Polly, the receptionist, informed me when she came back up from "The Parlour." Holding a packet of new tights in one hand, she handed them to me with a slight smile. "He asked if you could wear these for him."

I took the packet with curiosity and dashed off to the bathroom to put them on. Sitting perched on a chair in the corner, I began to roll my hold-ups off my legs.

"So you've got John then!" I looked up, puzzled, at Chloë, who was looking at the nude-coloured tights I had

---

*In 1997, the British pound (£) was worth approximately $1.70.

laid on the black-and-white tiled floor at my feet. She had been fixing her hair at the sink mirror. "Better not wear your knickers...He likes that best."

She looked back to the mirror, completely oblivious to the fact that I was wearing a lacy bodysuit.

Chloë was a sickly-thin short biker in her late thirties, with a long brunette mullet which constantly needed combing but looked a mess no matter what she did with it. Scarecrows had nothing on Chloë. She didn't get much work. One or two men would pick her, if she was lucky. She rushed off and wished me luck as a buzzer went. Putting my heels back on, I clipped the gusset of the bodysuit closed. Picking up some condoms from the box by the sink as I left, I put them in the pocket of the cheap, short leopard-print robe I had been given to wear over my "uniform" and wrapped it around me.

So this was it: after sitting around for a few hours and saying hello to a couple of men, my first shift was finally about to begin. All the girls' advice from earlier that morning was bouncing around in my head as I teetered down to the room. He was standing up at the foot of the bed when I knocked and walked in. He said hello and told me to take off the robe and my underwear, so he could see me in just the tights. I obliged. It was a surreal scene, light music playing in the background. Anything could have been playing for all I cared—I wasn't really listening.

I approached him, putting the rubbers on the bedside table. He was quite ordinary really, a ruddy, balding short guy with a pot belly. Turning me around, he stroked my encased bottom, down my legs, and around. He liked to rub me through the nylon, to make the fabric damp, he said. I had managed to suck a rubber on, as instructed, after reaching for it as he was on his knees sniffing at my behind. I was then asked quite politely to kneel on the bed on all fours. He positioned my bottom high in the air, took a deep sniff, and ripped a hole in the fabric for better access. It was all over in a few strokes and a shudder. At the last moment he whipped off the rubber and came all over my back. He said thanks and proceeded to have a shower; then it was my turn to wash away the stickiness he had left on me. After I had dried off and tidied up, he was ready to be shown out, fumbling a fiver into my palm as I stood at the door. It was all over in fifteen minutes flat! I saw him several times after that, but it never got any stranger—always the same routine, just different-coloured tights.

That was my first client: he knew exactly what he wanted, didn't take very long, and was polite. Still, a little disconcerting—I didn't know what to make of it. Up in the waiting lounge I had thought to myself: what am I going to do if they are all as weird as this? I asked Chloë whether they were all that bizarre. No, she reassured me—Mr. Tights Man was definitely one of the exceptions. My relief was short-lived when a few hours later a client notoriously known to the girls as Mr. Suck It Bitch summoned me to the Green Room. Again, I hadn't even said hello to him. Apparently, as a new girl, I had the privilege of being picked sight unseen.

Mr. Suck It Bitch came in twice a week—his wife was pregnant and otherwise occupied. Why "Suck It Bitch"? No one was forthcoming with the answer, but as I headed out of the lounge, I was assured that all would become clear by a girl who had just tottered by with the obligatory small plastic bundle of rubbish.

Mr. Suck It Bitch wasn't as bad as he sounded, a very presentable guy in his thirties, smart suit, and a bit of a laugh. Well, his thing, plain and simple, was a good hard blow-job, which was something I knew I did well. I didn't feel as nervous as I could have done. I still felt uneasy as I got to the end part of the massage—he really didn't seem to deserve the nasty tag the girls had given him, but what did I know, he was only my second client! He rolled off the bed and stood up as bold as brass at the side of the bed, his erection standing proud, hands on his hips. I sat there on the mattress with the condom in hand, tearing it open with nimble fingers and holding the rim; I pulled and sucked at the rubber surrounding him, all the while listening to his non-stop commentary, starting with a hearty "Ahhh..." and escalating to a cry of "Come on then, bitch. Suck it, bitch...Suck it, bitch..." OK, yep, I got it now. He forced my head down on him with his hands. Why do guys do that? I gagged time and time again as he sought to shove himself further down my throat.

Pulling out of his deep-throat exploit, he gasped and flipped me over so suddenly that I had hardly caught my breath before he plunged in between my legs and was in me up to the hilt. He was spent in one fell swoop and lay on top of me in a sweaty mess. Easing off me, he stretched like a pleased canine as I reached for the tissues to take off the condom and wipe him clean, depositing the rubbish in one of the small bags at the side of the bed.

"Marvellous...fucking marvellous," he groaned and, kissing me on the forehead, he bounded into the shower, leaving me to tidy up. Smiling as he emerged, I held a towel out for him and climbed under the still running water myself, to wash off his sweat, among other things.

As I rubbed down and adjusted my nylons, he slid a folded banknote into the top of my hold-ups as a tip as I sat on the bed. I was dressed and standing by the door by the time he finished tying his shoes, as there wasn't much for me to put on. He waved thanks at the back door as I showed him out and he left smiling. I, on the other hand, was thinking maybe I should leave now as, maybe, it would get worse. But I'm not a girl to give up, so I gathered my resolve as well as a handful of condoms and thought, Next!

My last client, late that night, was a Chinese man, up in the Velvet Room. He was very quiet. I walked over to the bed, where he was lying face down on the mattress. I sat by his side and tried to chat but his English was abysmal and we ended up exchanging crude hand signals. I gave him a back massage to start with and turned him over to rubber up. I was having a job to keep the condom on him as he was quite small. Not that I minded a small endowment at this stage, as I was feeling a bit raw and swollen from the two penetrations earlier on. With the rubber eventually on—sucking it on had really helped—he grew a little harder, sliding about in the latex. Standing up abruptly at the edge of the bed, he swung me on to my back to face him, pulling both of my legs off the bed. He pushed my knees up to my chest and, bending over me, he held my wrists above my head, swinging my left wrist over to join my right. He had entrapped both my hands in one of his so that he had one free to explore.

He sucked hard at each of my nipples in quick succession and then drew back and slapped my breasts playfully with his free hand, from left to right, until they turned pink...I didn't flinch as he fingered me either, probing further with his skinny digits. I was too busy trying to keep my wits about me and wasn't going to give him any indication that it hurt like hell, as he probably would have got off on it and gone on just to spite me—and the last thing I wanted was for it to continue any longer than it had to.

I wriggled my hands free, reaching down with one hand to hold the rubber in place on him. With that he plunged into me. While pushing me down into the bed, he tried to move my hand out of the way, but he soon came with a distraught grunt, disgruntled at his own loss of control. Phew, at least that was over. Didn't even let me wipe him off with a tissue as he let the filled rubber fall to the floor. Eweeeww, disgusting, and definitely hurt male pride! Served him right, ha. I eased myself up, my joints a bit stiff from being pinned down so forcefully. He thanked me with a brief nod, didn't shower, and got dressed in a hurry as I tidied up, picking up the disposed condom with a tissue and the paper bedroll used to protect the bed cover, putting it all into the little plastic rubbish bag. With the room ready for its next occupant, I showed him out the back door. No wave from him.

And that was my first shift over and done with...Phew! I didn't have to tip the receptionist as it was my first day. I had earned £70, which included the two £5 tips from Mr.

Tights Man and Mr. Suck It Bitch. It was nearly enough to pay my student rent for the month or for a third of my much-needed camera! All that for one day's work! For normal part-time work, I would probably have had to do three weekend shifts to earn the same amount, working more hours with less time to fit in my studies. When you start to weigh it up like that, going back for more becomes an easier prospect.

I was ordered a cab at the end of my shift as it was late, and was offered an all-day shift on Friday if I wanted to come back. I only had one class, which wasn't compulsory, so that was fine and I accepted. I felt shattered physically and mentally but was secretly glad that I had managed to do it. It had not been as scary as I had anticipated, everyone had been nice, if a little quiet, towards me, but I could under- stand that and was a little wary in return. I had felt safe, with the panic buttons in the rooms, and relieved at the high standard of hygiene. I spent the next few days nearly chick- ening out of going back, but the money was fantastic and the adrenaline rush was unlike anything I'd ever experi- enced. Unknowingly, I had already become hooked.

Vital Statistics

*B*efore I begin, sorry to ruin the media's stereotypical image of hookers, but I have never been abused by any member of my family or any ex-boyfriends. Nor have I *ever* taken drugs, alcohol, smoked anything, or self-harmed to get by. I would consider it a weakness in myself to inflict that kind of harm on my body and soul. So I suppose it sounds strange and contradictory that I ended up playing what is considered by many to be a dangerous game of Russian roulette with my sexual health. I try to be as careful as I can be, taking every precaution I can think of—which is a damn sight safer than most "normal" people I know on a "normal" night out. I suppose I have always had a high sex drive, and at least it keeps me out of the gym! I'm a bit bloody-minded actually, there's not much chance of making me do anything I don't want to do; I tend to dig my heels in and stand my ground, fighting all the way.

The main problem with people knowing what I do for a living is the automatic assumption that all my friends are involved in the sex industry, that I must be up to something naughty all the time, and that any bloke I sleep with has to pay me! The fact is that I hang around with more of my normal friends than any of the girls at work and have a great personal sex life that includes many people who don't give me money, when I can be bothered. Misconceptions and prejudice don't bother me in the slightest. In fact, I've only ever had one girl not talk to me after she found out how I earned my living. The way I look at it, if she's that narrow-minded, that is her problem. And as far as legalization goes, it is a completely grey area. The people who don't want the government to legalize brothels are, surprisingly, we in the industry! I am quite happy with the situation: I don't need the government to pimp me; I'm quite capable of doing that myself, thanks!

The fact is, the more sex I have, the more I crave it. I don't see it as an addiction—more of an indulgence. Everyone has a vice, it just happens that mine is sex. It's like being an athlete of sorts: the passion, the build-up, the mental focus and physical pursuit of a goal is like a sexual sport, and one I adore. I have tried not to be too graphic as I write, but the act is graphic, SEX is graphic...Making Love is a whole different ball game—indeed, having sex makes me appreciate Making Love. To me, it's not better or worse, just...different. I find great pleasure in both, depending on what mood I'm in and who I am with, of course!

Everyone has a skeleton in their closet, a dirty little secret—you know the one I mean. I don't feel ashamed of mine, just apprehensive about what I do. It's such a big taboo, but the general public are more accepting than you might think. People are always interested in the details—

not at first, when they find out what I do, but as it ticks over, they feel slightly ashamed to ask questions. I don't mind, as long as they are discreet and don't pussy-foot around me...Just ask and get it over with. I have got past the point of being embarrassed any more; there's not much that shocks me, I have been there and done it all before—probably!

Popping the Cherry: So Where Did It All Begin?

*I*t started a good six months earlier with my determination to get rid of my virginity, which actually wasn't as easy as it sounds. No matter what I did, I just couldn't seem to go all the way. It wasn't that I didn't want to, it just really hurt! My best friend Dee's advice proved to be very profound given how I now earn my living. She claimed, "The more you fuck, the easier it gets...but you've got to relax, babe." Wise words indeed. However, that was no consolation to me. I had been relaxed and I still had problems squeezing him in. It had been frustrating to say the least, painful to say the most. I soon became addicted to keeping an eye out for a suitable guy to help me with the deed. I wasn't going to let my sister lose it before me. At fifteen, she was five years younger than me with a steady boyfriend, and I was devastated to think that she might do it before me. Sure, there had been a few dates...but nothing more. It's not as though there was anything wrong with me, apart from my dark, sarcastic side. I'm five foot five, fit and toned with a curvy figure, long red hair (or, as everyone calls it, strawberry-blonde), blue-green eyes, pale skin, and a few freckles. In fact, quite cute really, if I do say so myself! Apart from, that is, my tiny 34AA tits— annoying when you consider that all the other females in my family have huge breasts. No one is under a C cup: even my little sis is bigger than me. As a kid, I wasn't a child who shone in any sense. My sister was the one who did that for the both of us. I was the quiet one, the one in class who no one would really notice. I wasn't popular but I was occasionally friends with the kids who were. But I wasn't a goodie two-shoes. I was the kid who kept her head down and got on with her work, the kid teachers forgot was there. Quite frankly, that was fine by me. I didn't want to stand out. I figured if you stood out, you made yourself a target.

It was quite evident, even when we were little, that my sister was blessed with the brains and I had been handed— well, the hands! I'm not putting myself down, it's just that I can't memorize pages of books and come out of exams with all A's like she could. I think, though, if I had a choice, I wouldn't swap my practical skills for academic ones. The practical ones are far more profitable if you use them to your advantage. And more fun.

At home, discipline was a major driving force. I worked out quite quickly that good girls got what they wanted and bad girls (my little sister being a whingeing, naughty example) got nowhere fast. In fact, if people thought you were good and you caused them no trouble, you could get away with most things. My sister, on the other hand, never got it and, although I love her to bits, by family consensus she's still a royal bossy pain in the ass. Takes after my father. What with that and the fact that my mother is partly dyslexic and has issues with thinking she's stupid, even though she's one feisty woman and no pushover, you have the perfect family cocktail for drama.

I was still living at home as my father was unemployed again (not for want of trying) and, as my parents could only just cover the mortgage, I was literally bringing in the money that fed us with my small full-time job in a garage (any leftovers being put straight into my uni fund). I didn't consider us poor, but I know my grandparents on both sides bailed us out on at least two occasions to stop our house from being repossessed. I love my family and didn't want to leave them or cause them any more financial grief. I'd talked this through with my cousin at one point, and she thought that I should leave home and get a flat of my own—they would cope—but I said that I wouldn't leave until my sister had finished school. Plus, at the time, I was happy enough where I was.

But there was one thing that was making me extremely dissatisfied—by the age of twenty, I felt truly inadequate as a woman. If I was so "beautiful," how come I didn't feel it, especially when I looked in the mirror and saw a twelve-year-old looking back? When I was a teenager many guys had flirted with me and asked me out but I had given them little consideration at the time as I was way too busy with work, my family, and sport to have any time for them. However, inadequacies and duty aside, I was going to be twenty-one in ten months for god's sake and hopefully not a virgin for very much longer...my fingers were crossed that it would happen soon (and only using my fingers to satisfy myself was making me extremely frustrated!).

I set about finding my experimental prey and soon enough located him at the local nightclub. A few of the guys at the gym I went to worked at the club on the door, so it was easy enough to get in, all the girls went there.

At twenty-eight he was tall and dark with nice broad shoulders. I will call him Patrick. I always have been a sucker for a nice back. Second on my list are guys who look like someone has hit them in the face with a spade. Pretty boys are just not my thing—you can take Brad Pitt and all the boy models and I will swap you for a boxer or a rugby player any day of the week. We chatted, flirting madly with each other. There was definitely chemistry between us—I fancied the pants off him. I buzzed with anticipation as we edged on to the packed dance floor, getting a little hot and sweaty with his hands all over me, running up and down my sides. Mine were just as busy over him, getting carried away and unbuttoning his shirt. I had got to the last button when I felt a tap on my shoulder.

I turned around, my back to my prospective lover. It was Mark, one of the security guards from the gym. How he had spotted us in the packed throng I don't know.

"Do his shirt up or I will have to throw a bucket of water over the two of you." He sounded serious.

"Christ, they're strict in here," my dance partner whispered in my ear as the two men eyeballed each other over my head. "No, just a tad over-protective," I muttered as I led him away from Mark and over to the bar.

At the end of the night we left the club together under the gaze of a huddled, black-suited group consisting of Mark and all the other doormen. What was their problem? Just because they called me the Ice Princess, that didn't make it true! I had found out about my label the week before, hearing it in passing. Hell, Mark was married and it was nothing to do with him anyway, but even though he was just an over-protective friend who flirted with me, he seemed to think he owned me. It was all very annoying.

I gave my new friend a lift as he was staying at a mate's house nearby. The comrade in question, having had no luck on the "pulling front," had left some time earlier in the evening. I had borrowed my parents' car for the night, and we sat outside his friend's place, chatting some more, not wanting the night to end. Well...he was dead cute and I so wanted to get in his trousers.

I told him I wasn't experienced and had been looking for someone to free me. Cheesy line, I know, but I had heard it in a movie somewhere and at that point it had sprung to mind. He was clearly flattered and, hand on my knee, told me if he did anything I didn't like he would stop. Well, I couldn't pass up that opportunity, could I? Here was a damn sexy guy willing to put out! So I drove further down the street to a dead-end lane and parked up. He pushed his chair back and I leaned over and sat on his lap. Kissing heavily while exploring each other, we slowly disrobed, discarding clothing rather awkwardly as the confines of a car are not really ideal, as anyone who's ever tried it knows.

My...he was a big boy! Just wrapping my fingers around it felt good—warm and smooth. I enclosed it with my mouth and sucked. I could tell from his intake of breath that he liked it, and he told me so. He made me stop before he came, said he could wait. Winding the driver's seat back flat, he placed me so I sat on the steering wheel, rather precariously, half on and half off. Luckily the car horn was in the central column and not on the rim I was sitting on, as I did not want to be interrupted by nosy neighbours at this point. Getting on all fours (not easy for a six foot guy in a small hatchback), he set me afire in an exploding wave of euphoria as he set about his task with his tongue. I was throbbing. It was fantastic.

I pounced on top of him after that, but he hugged me close. I started to fondle him but he grasped my hands and told me to stop. Hugging me to him, he kissed me, telling me he wanted the space and time to do it right. Next weekend perhaps? Great! I had managed to pick the only gentleman in the area! Typical! Frustrated wasn't the word.

To this day I still admire his restraint that early morning. I did feel a bit put out, though, as I dropped him off at his mate's having wiped the steamy windows down first. I drove home as the dawn was slowly breaking. I drove all the way without the radio on and, I remember, it was so eerily quiet. Creeping quietly to my bed so my parents wouldn't notice how late I had come back, I had at least the knowledge that, next weekend, my virginity would be at an end. Wouldn't it?

He had a boat in dry dock—well, if you call his father's scrapyard, littered with cars, trucks, and buses, a dry dock. More like a vehicular graveyard. It was Patrick's passion to fix big boys' toys, being an extremely capable managing engineer at one of the top car manufacturers in the country. Amazingly dextrous hands, he had…sends me all aquiver just thinking about them, even now!

His favourite toy at the time, a humungous, tan-coloured, state-of-the-art Range-Rover-type thing which was taken on dune-racing expeditions to God only knows where abroad, was parked in pride of place. As you drove in, you couldn't miss it. His darling vehicle had swallowed every penny he had, to the point where he couldn't afford to buy a place to live, and was currently single. His long-suffering fiancée had been at her wits' end, wanting to get married and set up home, and when it clearly wasn't going to happen any time soon, she had eventually kicked him out. So, having nowhere else to go, he had moved back in with his mum and dad, sleeping weekends on his old toy, the sparkling, reconditioned, cabined motor boat at one end of his father's scrapyard.

This is where we had arranged to meet, after spending many hours that long week on the phone flirting and talking dirty. I had driven down the coast and parked in his yard. It was a calm summer Saturday afternoon. He was sitting there, a six-pack in shorts, on the deck of his one-berth boat, swinging his legs and bare feet over the side, watching me arrive in my dad's car. He helped pull me aboard, my small bag swung over my shoulder, and grasping my jean-clad bottom, he held me to him, whispering in my ear that he had been dreaming of my lips around him all week.

Letting me go, he ushered me below deck. It was empty apart from a raised foam-padded base-sheet cover which took up the front half of the small vessel. After shedding the little clothing we had on, some serious groping, rubbing, and rolling around progressed. Eventually I was sprawled naked beneath him—we had hardly spoken since I had boarded. Some time later, hot and sweaty, I was desperately ready for him, but I was only to be thwarted when he could not even enter me. Great...wonderful...not again! Drawing my legs up towards my chest, he peered at me for a moment, then turned me about-face with a greedy grin of desire, and we tried to ease the problem by taking our time in a 69.

The sun was setting by then, bathing the cabin in a golden glow. My, that sounds so romantic, and it sort of was, until, stretching, I noticed a glint on the floor—a pair of handcuffs poking out of his discarded shorts pocket. Ehh? Bending down, I picked them up and placed the cold metal on his stomach, which startled him. With big, puppy-dog brown eyes he looked up at me and murmured coyly, "Oh, yeah...Umm...Only if you want to wear them..."

Curling up next to him, I purred in his ear, "You don't need to cuff me...I am not going anywhere," as I toyed with the cuffs on his chest. By now I trusted him not to harm me. The measure of his restraint was amazing; I knew he would stop and uncuff me if I asked him to. If that sort of thing turned him on, it was the least I could do: I was feeling a bit of a failure for not being able to put out and all.

We tried again, this time with me cuffed under him, hands above my head holding the keys. I am not daft—he could still have done anything to me—but I convinced myself that if I held the keys it would be OK.

I wanted to put my hands on him, to stroke him, as his head was in my lap. Not losing the keys was all I could think about at that point so, with something of a struggle, I fumbled with them in a way which would have made Houdini proud, undid the cuffs, and rolled him beneath me. Sitting on his legs, I rolled down a rubber and gave him a few sucks before trying to slide down his length very slowly. No go. Clams had nothing on me!

It must have been around midnight that I awoke and, wriggling against him, I soon had him aroused and rubber-coated. It was a warm night in the yard, pitch-black, and we were soon on the deck, the cuffs swinging on the tip of his finger as he led me by the hand to the side rail.

Bent over, handcuffed to the deck railing, I held on to the cool metal with both hands. I looked down as he worked with his fingers, bent over with his body up against my back. He tried to ease into me and I gritted my teeth, hoping this time it would be easier. I took a deep breath as he pushed in gently, stopping half his length to see if I was OK. Why the hell was I so tight? This was slightly painful but I was still shaking from the effect of his fingers, so I pushed back on to him, my eyes watering as I did so. He only moved a couple of strokes before he could go no further, so after uncuffing me he carried me below, laying me down on the crumpled sheets.

My body had let me down! I had seized up again! The swelling was stopping him from entering me. I was devastated. But at least now I was not a virgin any more, which was some consolation, although I was all the more frustrated now I had glimpsed what I'd been missing!

He said maybe I needed to relax some more and try when the swelling went down. He stroked and massaged me from head to foot as we talked, which inevitably turned into playing and fondling each other. I sucked him, as he was extremely hard, and had to finish him off by hand. Good job I had brought tissues in my bag...messy boy!

Drowsily awakening at dawn, I felt him stir on my behind as we were spooned together. With his arms around me, I turned over and he kissed my forehead asking if I was OK. Not totally awake, I nodded and stroked the hard lump between us, and not feeling so swollen myself, I pushed him down against the mattress, dressed his member, and slid on top slowly, easing down on him an inch at a time, still an extremely tight fit and slightly uncomfortable. He groaned, putting his hands on my hips, lifting me and sliding me down to the base again. Pins and needles ran up my spine. I must have looked as if I was in pain, which I was, so he drew me down to him and held me to his chest. There I lay with him in me, rocking back and forth. Pulling out, he stroked me as I finished him off. I left later that morning for the warmth and comfort of home, hungry for breakfast and wanting a shower, as there was no galley or bathroom on board. Peeing in bushes is not fun at the best of times, but in the semi-darkness with stinging nettles nearby is not something I would recommend. Toilets are a wonderful invention and padded toilet roll even better.

Swollen now, I climbed down the ladder, waving goodbye to him as he stood proud and naked on the deck. The elation of no longer being a supposedly frigid ice maiden didn't last for long. Feeling let down, I was blaming myself for my bodily barriers.

It was very late on the Sunday afternoon the following day. After our morning training session at the club, Dee and I had stumbled wobbly-legged into her local. She was looking out of the window at the boats jostling in the harbour. The faint clanking from the mast lines was distracting me through the open window. Taking up the line she had thrown at me—"The more you fuck, the easier it gets...but you've got to relax, babe"—I turned her way.

"So what do you suggest...I work in a brothel for practice and dope myself up beforehand to relax till I can shag normally?"

"Not quite what I meant," she said, raising her eyebrows at me. Little did I know how ironic that throwaway comment would turn out to be.

Bordello Life Begins

September marked the beginning of my university career and a whole new chapter in many other ways. Suddenly, rather than lectures and seminars, hanging out with other art students, I found myself liaising with the likes of Mr. Suck It Bitch. How did I get here?

The reality was, I was a student living away from home for the first time, just about able to pay the rent but with no long-term financial plan. I had started my classes four weeks earlier. I've always seemed to excel in art and have a deep passion for the subject in any form. It's hands on, it's messy—what more could I need? Travel? Well, the upcoming art-department trip to Venice was planned for six months' time and I really wanted to go. I had always dreamed of going to Venice. I love travel but, this time, it meant I needed a good camera—and the cash to get one! You can't go to a place filled with as much art and history as Venice and not record it.

Having saved from my previous job, I had enough money to cover my rent and food for most of my foundation year, but what I hadn't planned on was the exorbitant cost of supplies, books, fees, etc., that came with the course. The government had abolished student grants the year before and I hadn't wanted to get a student loan like everyone else and be in mounting debt for years after (2.6 percent interest when I read the small print—I didn't care what anyone said, no matter how you look at it, 2.6 percent is not a straight-off loan). I only applied for one because my family said I should, but I ended up giving it all back when it came through as I couldn't stand the thought that I owed the government a penny. I don't like to owe money, that's the kind of person I am. My cousin Cal had been left with a £12,000 debt after she finished her education, and it was the scandal of the family. I so did not want that hanging over me. As kids, Cal was always saving up to buy computer games and she asked what I was saving for when she heard I was putting my birthday money in the bank. I said I was just saving. I loved seeing it tally up in my bank book as a child. It's sad, but I still do.

Money, for me, spells freedom. Freedom to go where you wish, do what you wish. Everyone always wants more money—it's human nature—but I don't just want it now. I am by nature a very patient person. I can wait, plan, and nurture those plans until it's definitely all mine. A bit calculating? Probably. But making money, I have found, is something, like sex, that I do well.

If I wanted to pay the rent, go to Venice, and have a good camera to record the trip, there was only one thing for it—the dreaded Part-Time Student Job. Money from a part-time job would help fund the trip and mean that I would not have to dip into my savings for accommodation and food. It's not as though I could ask my family for financial help—they needed every penny to keep afloat, as my father had just been made redundant yet again. The problem was finding something that I wanted to do. Reading through the job section of the local paper was the first thing I did. No point in looking in the second-hand section for a camera—I had made up my mind that if I was going to buy one, I might as well have a brand-new one with up-to-date features. As I scanned the local paper's job section over a cup of tea in the cold student-dorm kitchen, something stood out: the massage parlour/sauna at the bottom of the road was hiring. It was a dodgy-looking place and I had walked past it several times without really paying much attention. It was extremely clean, though, with shiny, blacked-out windows, a red canopy, and gold letters. I was intrigued. Everyone knew it was a brothel and it was common knowledge up and down the uni halls. I naïvely thought that perhaps I could just do massage and blow-jobs, as I knew I did those well. But, still having a craving for sex, I thought if I could just get the less endowed guys I would not have a problem. Also, I was just plain curious and wouldn't be able to stop myself from going all the way!

Wrestling with my mind is never a good thing—a certain part of my anatomy will overrule my head and my heart if I'm not careful. The massage job would solve a few of my problems in one hit, money in my pocket for a new camera and help with the rent, for a start. This little job on the side would mean that I could have more freedom with the added bonus of trying to sort out my horny little problem...

There was the risk element, not to mention nerves...OK, I was scared to death. I am a bit of a wuss, but not so much so when I have balanced out the pros and cons. I naïvely thought not much could happen to me—I couldn't get into that much trouble, could I? It was a business advertising in the paper and based only a stone's throw from the local cop shop, so surely if it was bad news it would have been busted by now?

I was fit and fairly strong, even if I hadn't been to the gym in a while. If I got there and didn't like it I could leave, and there was always the police station down the end of the road, so I could make a run for it. I also have the advantage that I don't look like I could hurt a fly but actually I can topple a guy with one hell of an up-and-under rugby tackle to the knees—the guys at the gym taught me that one, along with some other self-defence, so I have never really felt physically threatened even though I am small. I will talk my way out of problems if I can, though, rather than scarper.

In my room the next day I looked at all the other ads again but still came back to the one I had circled. The other part-time student-job stuff wouldn't give me time for my studies, surely? And this did, on the surface, look as if it would pay well. At the weekend I walked down the road, passing the place by a few times. I stood a way off at a bus stop to see if anyone came in or out. Half an hour went by and no one had gone in or come out, so I walked past again and went back to my pokey little room to read up on some classwork books.

I phoned the number after a week of thinking about the ad some more and a further good half-hour of hovering by the phone in the dorm hallway nursing a cup of tea, largely because I was nervous but mainly because I wanted to make sure the coast was clear.

I made the call. The phone was picked up abruptly on the second ring. As she rattled off "Hello, how can I help you?" in my ear, I took a deep breath. "I read your ad in the paper. Are you taking on any girls?" Phew, that wasn't too hard. A bit rushed and a bit hushed but at least she heard me.

I was asked by the pleasant lady on the other end if I "knew what was involved." I said I had a fair idea. Cripes, I hoped I did. I was promptly told that interviews were held on a walk-in basis between two and five in the afternoon any day, and I could pop in for a chat—no pressure—and leave if it wasn't for me. "See you soon" was the last thing she said, in her chirpy little voice, and then she was gone, leaving me hanging up the phone and gagging for a fresh cuppa to still my nerves.

A couple of days later, I took a long look at my bank statements and at the cork board in my room with its pinned-on shrine to all things Venetian. It certainly helped me to work up the courage. I headed down the street and rang the buzzer spot on 2 p.m. It was now or never. I ducked into the doorway, standing there on the step in my jeans, T-shirt, and smart shoes. With my hair loose I felt less conspicuous, as I usually wore it up, out of the way. I wore a long red baggy jacket down to my knees—not something I was usually seen in, I just hoped that if someone spotted me in passing, they wouldn't recognize me. So, huddled at the door, I pressed the buzzer. It clicked straight away so I pushed it open and headed up the stairs in front of me. At least I didn't have to wait on the doorstep—I felt really obvious in a big red coat as it was.

At the top of the stairs there was a corridor to the left, bending around the corner out of sight. The right side opened up into a waiting room, with a large wooden desk, its surface empty apart from a telephone, with a chair tucked neatly underneath. Music was playing softly in the background and the place felt warm and cosy, with subtle lighting and fake plants. I sat on one of the big, plush sofas pushed up against the large window facing the desk and waited nervously for what was a long eight minutes.

Looking at my foot tapping on the red carpet gave me focus. The cream walls were adorned with large reproductions of classic nudes in big gilt-effect frames. The windows behind me looked down on to the street below, or would have if the ruffled blinds drawn over them had not blocked out the smallest glimpse of sunlight. The windows themselves were dramatic, framed theatrically with long Victorian-style tasselled gold and dark red drapes. Everything set the tone: the house looked like the quintessential French bordello.

The receptionist, Cebell, a woman of medium build with mid-length, straight blonde hair and a fringe, was in her late thirties. She bustled towards me along the corridor, explaining that she was so sorry, but when she looked at the door camera, she had thought I was Carry, one of the other girls. We had almost identical hair and on a small screen it was easy to mistake us, that's why she had simply buzzed me in. She had only come out to investigate when Carry had appeared at the back door on a different camera a few minutes later.

I don't think she even took a breath while shaking my hand, she talked that much. After answering the phone, she ushered me to another room down the corridor, very similar to the first but much smaller, with one sofa and a chair. Cebell gestured to the chair and asked if I wanted a drink. I declined.

A more formidable lady with short red hair swept through the door and threw herself on to the sofa, making the room seem very cramped. It was one of the owners: Mrs. Boss. "Coffee," she smiled from the sofa to Cebell as the recep nodded and left the room.

I found out much later that girls who turned up for interview who were deemed too old, out of shape, or just plain ugly were turned away in the front sitting room with "I'm sorry, but at present we don't need any other girls, but we'll ring you if we do," which basically is a load of bull, as a house always needs girls; it was just a polite way of saying thanks but no thanks. The candidates who passed the recep's once-over were taken to a smaller greeting room to be interviewed and have the rules explained to them by the receptionist. I, it seemed, had been graced with the appearance of Mrs. Boss.

I learned even later that Mrs. B hardly ever interviewed unless she thought you would be a good addition to the house and so didn't want to lose your interest or scare you off with the brief interview the receps gave. She ran the house with her partner, Mr. B, who was not present and hardly had any say in the day-to-day business. The interview involved her giving as much info as you needed to make your decision and an opportunity to ask questions;

there wasn't any stripping or intimate probing into your love life at all, which made me feel more comfortable.

Mrs. B had worked out of a flat as a girl herself for many years and had now set up on a bigger scale as a Madam, she informed me rather proudly. The "sauna" had been running for a year and a half. I was introduced to Kerry, and shown around by her, but I couldn't go into the girls' lounge as one of the girls from my university was working that day and was in there at the time. If I decided not to call back and accept the job, it could have been awkward for her, my knowing what she did. It was nice to know they would take the same kind of care of my identity.

Another good thing was that you didn't have to do anything or go with anyone you were unhappy with, and that extended to the guys who picked you from the line-up. If you didn't want to see a client, that was fair enough. It was slightly frowned upon if you didn't have a good reason, but if you weren't happy about it, that was it. If you went to a room and took an instant dislike to someone before anything happened, all you had to do was make a polite retreat to the girls' lounge, no questions asked, and the receptionist on duty would send another girl instead. I never retreated, however, priding myself on taking the rough with the smooth. It was only thirty minutes, after all; if you were lucky, it was over in five.

The house having proved a great success, it was now being expanded to include three reception rooms, seven bedrooms, a sauna, and a four-person jacuzzi. There was a big girls' TV lounge, a fully stocked kitchen, and a bathroom/changing room with boxes of condoms, stockings, and a rail of outfits. The house was a maze of a place, on three levels with winding corridors. Kerry showed me all over, tripping up and down steps in her leopard-print robe as she did so. There was the main door, and the back door, which the girls and the gentlemen who needed a more discreet entrance used. As I walked the corridors to and from the rooms, I became aware of the distinctive odours of cigarette smoke and air freshener and of a musty smell, which I can only describe as the smell of sex, which permeated the house. The girls' waiting lounge, on the other hand, just smelled of cigarettes.

The rooms, seven in all, were comfortably warm and scrupulously clean, most with shower cubical, water cooler, TV, and sofa, and a coffee table if there was room for one. This would be laden with flavoured bottled water and an ashtray. The big double beds had small side tables with baby oil, talc, tissues, folded paper bedroll, air freshener, and a box of small bags for rubbish. Porn was relayed to every room from the lounge video-player, the tapes bought from abroad, mostly Germany, by Mr. B, I was duly informed. Kerry's blonde ringlets bounced as she nodded, smiling away, explaining it all. All I could think at the time was how Kerry could manage to bounce away on a client without getting her huge hooped earrings caught up in all that hair.

The largest room was the Ballroom. This was the only room with disabled access from the back of the building. It was very dark, high-ceilinged, with a bath. It was huge and because of this was always a tad chilly. The Velvet Room was the only room at the top of the building and had a large wall mirror behind the bed and a corner bathtub that took ages to fill. The Mirror Room was all black with mirrored walls, mirror tiles above the bed, a chair, and a bath. It was the only room with a toilet.

The Parlour was the most popular room as it was the most comfortable; it was downstairs and at the other end of the corridor from the sauna and jacuzzi. Next to it was the Green Room, virtually identical, but slightly smaller and also with a TV playing porn. Then there was the Ruby Room, a tiny space with everything crammed in, and the Yellow Room, on the floor directly above it. Next to the Yellow Room were the two gents' loos.

At first it was confusing for me simply finding my way around! Keeps you damn fit running up and down all those stairs in stilettos. Even in bare feet, I always run upstairs on my toes now through sheer habit.

It felt too good to be true. A clean, friendly, well-run house? Where was the shabby furniture, the dark, damp, seedy rooms? The junkie girls forced to work by pimps? They were nowhere to be seen. You see it all on TV, in movies, and in the press and I had all these misconceptions in my head. However, I soon realized that I had totally landed on my feet and had no hesitation in accepting the job that Mrs. B formally offered me at the end of my interview and tour. I was now employed.

Learning the Ropes

I have always been told I am blessed by the luck gene and, sure enough, this happened to be the best house to work in, as I found out a few days later when I was talking to the contented girls who worked there. House rules dictated that all the girls work two shifts a week. A shift started at 10:30 a.m. and normally finished at 1 a.m., or later if men were still coming in. You could do a half shift, finishing or starting at 6 p.m., but most girls worked a whole shift—they earned more that way because it was busier later on in the evening. Five of us worked during the day and two others would start at 6 p.m., making our number seven at night. If you needed extra money you could ask for an extra shift and they would try and fit you into the rota.

The clients would arrive, pick a girl, and pay £40 for half an hour to the receptionist. The chosen girl would get £20 (plus any tips), and the rest went to the house. Apart, that is, from the £10 house fee we paid out of our money to the receptionist for half a shift. You were only exempt from this charge if you were filling in for a girl taking a sick day. The other charge occurred if you were more than ten minutes late—then you had a £10 fine to pay. I was only ever late in once, because I overslept. The majority of the time I was in early, normally the first girl on the doorstep, as I lived practically round the corner.

A Gemini half-hour was £50 for the company of two girls, for which each girl got £15 and the house got £20. A thirty-minute "Show," which was a girl-on-girl lesbian act, was £100. Not everyone was up for it and I only did it after a few months, when I got to know the girls better.

If the client was feeling energetic he could go for a Double Decker, which was one girl for half an hour followed by another girl for another half an hour straight after. Each girl got £20, but the house got £30, making it a £70 fee. There was also the option for a client to pick two girls to join him in the jacuzzi for ten minutes—after that he'd pick one girl to take upstairs. Each girl got £5, even if you weren't picked for the full service.

Confused? Well I was, as I listened and nodded. OK so far. The house also had an offer for the regulars: each time they came in, they requested their card, it got marked for each visit and placed back in the Rolodex. When they had been in ten times they got the next "massage" half price. We girls got the normal £20 for this, but the house made nothing. It doesn't sound much, £20 for doing a half-hour full service, but when your rent is only £30 a week you're laughing all the way to the bank.

We were paid at the end of the night when the chart was tallied up, which was good as you didn't have to worry that one of the less scrupulous girls would take your money from your bag when you were, as it were, occupied.

If you needed food during the day, there was a fully stocked fridge and freezer and soft drinks in a cupboard. The freezer was restocked on a Sunday morning when the local superstore would send a delivery of frozen packages via the Freezer Man, a very cheerful chap of quiet disposition, all eyes...Not that there was much to look at, with us wrapped up in our dressing-gowns, but still, he said our delivery was always the highlight of his working week. When questioned by a few of us, as we were surprised that he never came in to visit any of the girls for a massage, he would always say he would be too shy and then trundle off with his trolley, a bit pink but with a big grin on his face.

There was never any booze stocked in the kitchen or anywhere else on the premises: it wasn't allowed, not even for the clients, and neither were drugs—if you were found with either you would lose your job. It was a lot of information to take in. I was rather blown away when all this was explained to me, so I just sat and listened.

Other sackable offences included giving your number to clients, doing anal and unprotected oral for an extra cash tip (extras). Condoms were to be used at all times for sex and oral. This was the most important house rule and to this day I still love to suck cock encased in rubber, although now I use flavoured, as the noxill-9 spermicide makes your mouth numb. Have I said how obsessed I am with rubber? The smooth texture, the little squeaks it makes on my teeth as I suck it—and don't get me started on the flavoured ones, mint, and now vanilla my favourite...gives me shivers thinking of the taste. Letting a man go down on you was another no-no, and kissing was a big faux pas. To be truthful, I wasn't really bothered, but I preferred not to do either, not because I didn't want to, but in thirty minutes, who really has the time to mess around like that? There was never really an issue if I redirected the attention to a different, more fulfilling area—well, apart from the problem of drunken guys on late weekend nights who would slobber all over you and couldn't get it up. Reality is, it doesn't matter how good someone is at licking pussy or how many times it makes me come—I have a vibrator for that. Give me a good hard cock fuck any day and it will leave a smile on my face from ear to ear.

But I digress...back to the bordello I go.

With the trip to Venice at the forefront of my mind and my cash-for-camera fund non-existent after all the art-supply costs, the next day I called to apply for a shift. I was apprehensive and it must have shown in my voice as I was given a slow Monday-night shift to start with. I've known them to stick cocky new girls right in at the deep end on a Saturday night if they aren't too sure of their earning potential, just to see how they cope. I didn't know how lucky I was at the time. They were easing me in gently now I look back on it, with my first shift. Mrs. B must have seen pound signs looming and wanted to keep me interested and happy.

Because I was the new girl only a couple of the other girls spoke to me. Polly, the receptionist on my first day, explained that new faces appeared and then disappeared all the time as the new girls who couldn't hack it left, so some of the girls who had been there a while—the "older" girls—just would not make friends until they knew you were going to stick around. It was just too much effort when one in three girls left after their first shift. Fair enough, I got it—a case of sink or swim, or to put it another way, fuck or fuck off.

I don't think I had even taken my coat off when one of the girls sat me down in the kitchen and explained what to do in the room when I arrived for my Monday-evening shift. I just sat there in the kitchen fascinated as Carry the Redhead (the girl I had been mistaken for when they had buzzed me in for my interview) chatted away. I was so nervous, just concentrating on paying attention to what I was told. I found out later that Carry liked explaining all the goings-on to the new girls. A tall, leggy woman with the most amazing green eyes I had ever seen, she was our resident shrink, training to be a psychologist specializing in sex therapy. She would have made a good social worker, come to think of it. She was working at the house while studying and was dead useful for all sorts of random infor-mation, which normally spilled out as she was reading some huge textbook over a cup of tea and a packet of Hobnobs. Ironic choice of bickie, I know, but Hobnobs they were. "Do you want a Nob?" need only be said by Carry in a straight voice to have us tittering. I am sure she was doing the occasional case study on us as well as on her clients, but she kept it all very discreet and never pried too much so no one was too worried. What a way to do your research and get paid at the same time!

The main in-house training initiation was nothing sexual; in fact, it's all rather dull in real life. Most of what you learn is on the job if you stick the first few weeks, and really, you'll never know everything—you are always learning.

Carry was called away and others drifted in to fill her place and took over chatting and showing me the ropes. Training consisted mainly of how to put a condom on more safely than the roll-down method. It was safer because, if you had been using your hand to get the penis hard enough to roll the rubber on, then your hand or hands could have picked up any bacteria from him and wiped it on the outside of the rubber which was going to go in you. They showed me on a can of mousse how to take the rubber out of the packet holding the rim, then suck on the teat end and, with three fingers from both hands, roll and pull it down from the inside. This is supposedly where the myth of putting on a condom with just your mouth originated, mainly because you can do it so quickly and efficiently that most men don't realize what's going on and think you have just sucked it on. In real life this is only slightly possible if you are going to risk swallowing it, or if he can hold an erection long enough for you to faff about trying to get it on correctly with just your mouth. Ha! Like that's going to happen.

After many tries and a lot of practice, I could do it the way I was shown. I refined it over the weeks until I could put one on even a limp member in five seconds flat. Saves a lot of time that way, putting it on when they are soft—as soon as it's on you can suck it hard. Saves all the hand jobs, then the subsequent droop by the time you have rolled it down. Some guys wouldn't even know you had put it on if you started sucking really hard and fast—you would have them up in no time—the skill was judging when to stop in time to sit on and ride! Girls, if you are going to follow this advice, be careful—not all men are the same: some are very sensitive boys and need you to go slow. Some don't like a strong suck at all, and in very rare cases they can find it extremely painful. Thinking back to life before the house, I tried to remember the sensitive ones—it was hard to categorize as, to be honest, I had always been pretty good at blow-jobs (even when still a virgin). Thank God, as more often than not it was the guy's only consolation prize, as I was so tight until I lost my cherry with Patrick. Full sex was the last thing on the menu. Compensation sucking, in those early days, certainly came in handy, and in that frustrating situation, I rarely got any complaints for going too fast! Patrick certainly didn't mind—I'll never forget him lying back panting, his eyes shut, and murmuring, "I've needed that all week...mind-blowing. How you give such good head being a virgin is beyond me." That comment still makes me smile—no training, no diagrams in books, just pure instinct. But in the house, a blow-job was not the consolation prize I had been used to dishing out, it was an essential part of the procedure, and that meant that there were rules. Right-hand/left-hand use was also mentioned in passing, by Chloë. The consensus of the house was that you used your watch hand to touch yourself and the other hand to touch his bits. It was cleaner that way and easy to remember so you didn't get muddled up. Slightly difficult if you're ambidextrous, like I am, and put your watch on either wrist, though. I started to wear my watch on my left, as the right was my strongest "hand-shandy" hand...you go through a lot, but nothing too big as it can get in the way...yes, I mean the watch.

The receptionists were the backbone of the house and were pretty constant. They welcomed the clients, took the phone calls, did the laundry, and handled any trouble, which normally consisted of drunks late at night. Polly was a cheery lady, tall, thin, with curly blonde hair. She was always happy but could be a little dizzy at times. I enjoyed working when Polly was on as it was always a relaxed sort of day. She worked only on Mondays, Tuesdays, and Wednesdays but would on occasion take sporadic days off. She was in good shape for her age and looked so much younger that we didn't believe her when she had her forty-fifth birthday.

Louise was a little sterner than the other two reception-ists. She was of medium height with long dark hair, in her thirties, and took no shit from anyone. You didn't even try to win a verbal fight with Louise; you would always lose. She worked the busiest shifts, which were on Thursdays, Fridays, and Saturdays.

Cebell had a huge chest and was a bit dithery. Case in point: she was the one who'd let me in by mistake on my first day. She was a friend of Mrs. B's and would cover on Sundays and any other days when someone was needed to stand in. She was OK, but I don't think Mr. B liked her working on reception—any problems that kicked off always seemed to happen on one of her shifts.

When the doorbell rang the receptionist on duty greeted the client and showed him to one of the reception rooms, making him a drink if he wanted one. She would come back to her desk and press the desk buzzer, which could only be heard in the girls' lounge, kitchen, and girls' bathroom. This was the call that we were to get up and get ready in a line, then she would send us in one at a time to say our Kinky Hello, as our meet-and-greet was called. One girl in particular would rush into the kitchen and rub ice cubes on her nipples to make them perky. She thought it helped, as she had big nipples that would stand proud and say hello. It was an education to watch!

Walking into one of the small reception rooms, most girls would appear framed in the doorway like an unenthusiastic magician's assistant, all big hair and fake smile, and in the blink of an eye disappear just as quickly in a *poof* of cheap perfume. You had to stand at the doorway, say hello and give your name, then leave for the next girl to do the same. You get used to standing there on the threshold in just your underwear, hold-ups, and stilettos, saying hello to countless blank male faces over and over again. After a while it's a bit like going to the supermarket and not noticing the person on the check-out. However, it was bloody hard to start with—something I identified when I wasn't getting picked. Looks like I had beginner's luck with Mr. Tights Man, Mr. Suck It Bitch, and my Chinese guy. Polly explained it was because I looked so nervous and pale. She suggested a cup of tea, although I certainly remember being far from convinced that that would do the trick!

It took a while for me to get the hang of it, but I eventually became a pro when it came to saying, "Hello. Nice to meet you. My name is—" really slowly so the man could get a good look and a chance to remember my name, looking only into their eyes as I greeted them. I would trail slowly out—my bum was my best feature, after all! It was normally a surprise to see who had picked me after the line-up.

The receptionist would usher a client to one of the rooms when he had picked a girl. She would tell him to shower, lie down, and that the lady would be with him shortly. Like all the girls, I would give the guy at least five minutes to have a shower—any less than that and he might try to drag you in with him and you really don't have time for that nonsense. It would also mess up your hair and make-up, which you really, really don't have time for on a busy day. I would pick up any supplies that I needed (condoms and lube) and get the receptionist to note the time on the chart, then I would head to the room I had been assigned.

That's when the fun would start.

The Routine

$\mathcal{I}$ would normally enter the room to find a damp, naked body stretched out, face down on the bed. The shyer guys would be lying there with a towel around their hips. I would give my client a five-minute massage (slightly longer if he was enjoying it), then take off my underwear, turn him over, and take the condom from the top of my stocking hold-ups. I would sit astride his legs facing him while I put on the rubber ready to start the blow-job and suck him till he was good and hard. In this position he could not do the sharp, poking, trying-to-stick-his-fingers-up-me thing. The more adventurous ones would also be restricted from trying to sneak a finger up my behind. It's too small a hole, too painful (I don't like pain), and, more importantly, I don't have a prostate G-spot to excite! I don't go sticking things up guys' asses, unless they want me to and they ask nicely! So I think I should be afforded at least the same respect. If that was what I wanted, I would ask, thanks!

I would follow the blow-job by sitting on top (hopefully a nice hard member) and riding him till he came. I would hopefully time it so that I finished five minutes before time was up. He could then have an unhurried shower as I tidied up. This involved taking up the towel and paper bedroll strip. This was then replaced, the bedroll tucked under the towel at each end (making sure that the bedsheet was protected as well) ready for the next guest. Waiting for the showered client to dress, I would have a shower myself, quickly dry off as he was still dressing, pull on my robe, put any unused condoms back in my pocket, pick up waste/towels, and wait by the door with a smile ready to open it when he had finished putting on his shoes. If he took his time showering and the thirty minutes was up, I would go upstairs to have a shower in the girls' bathroom, then go back a few minutes later to show him out. If I stayed to tidy up whilst he was in the shower, he'd be ready for another go and I'd never get him out of the door!

I always took a quick look outside the door to make sure there was no one there to see the client leaving—clients tend not to like passing other guys in hallways; they might all be there for the same thing, but they still want to be discreet. It was a big house so it was very rare that a guy would bump into another unless it was a particularly busy day and the reception rooms were all full. In that event, the gents would have to wait on one of the sofas in the corridors.

When the coast was clear I would ask whether he would like to leave via the front or the back. Most gents would want to leave by the back door so, tottering upstairs and around corners, I would lead them to the exit, always keeping a look-out, then open the door and wave them off. On my way back to the girls' lounge, I'd stop by the recep's desk to make sure she noted my time out on the clipboard chart. After that, I would head to the bathroom and dump all my rubbish before making a nice cup of tea and catching up with whoever was in the lounge. All rubbish from any session went in the small plastic bags kept in the room and were taken up with the wet towels. The towels were deposited in the laundry "fluffer room," the rubbish in the girls' big bathroom bin.

If it was a really busy day, you just had time for a quick once-over in the mirror and then it was straight out to say hello to the next one waiting in the reception room or on one of the couches in the corridor. If you had time, it was great to redo your hair and make-up, go to the loo, put the kettle on for a cup of tea, and if it was really quiet, you could grab something to eat and kick your heels off—maybe even do some studying.

That was the normal routine, simple and easy if you were lucky.

Being late out of a room got you into trouble. The receptionist on duty would knock on the door, tell you time had run out, and ask you to leave the room—although, sometimes, the knock at the door was a godsend, especially if you were dealing with a drunk who couldn't get it up and was messing you around...a "droopy wanker." He might feel horny and be able to get the old boy up, but would he be able to do the business with all that alcohol swishing about? I would always advise turning up before meeting the friends at the pub. A Yo-Yo dick is a real tease; it's disheartening and frustrating to get a girl all worked up and then not be able to deliver—a bit of an insult, quite frankly.

Mr. and Mrs. B were a nice couple and they weren't stupid, either. They knew that as long as the girls were happy, the clients left happy, came back, and told friends; ergo, more clients, more money for the house and for them.

We even had use of a lawyer and an accountant to help us out with problems if the need arose. Also, if a girl was having a particularly bad week, Mrs. B would give her a present of a beauty treatment to cheer her up. She wasn't daft; outward appearance and liveliness were everything, that's why you got picked. That's how we all made money.

Presentation was key, and this also applied to the house. The decor of the whole building would change every couple of months. Mrs. B said she liked the place to be kept fresh and in good order—it was essential for business, I was briskly informed. The house went through a lot of mattresses, I can tell you—that place would be a great test-centre for bed-mattress companies!

The decor was not the only thing that was forever changing. There was the never-ending towel-fluffing. The "fluffing room" (sounds like some seventies porn set, I know) was a big towel laundry behind the kitchen. The two washing machines were constantly on the go, so there were always plenty of towels to fold, giving a whole different meaning to the word "fluffer"! A specific three-fold method was used, so they all were neatly folded the same (mainly to hide the fact that some were well used and thready around the edges). They were then stored on waist-high slatted wooden shelving units which filled the walls of the girls' waiting lounge. Each unit was labelled with the name of the room in which the towels belonged, with different colours for each room. Towels were taken down to stock the rooms along with anything else that was needed.

Helping the receptionist to fold towels every now and then was a good way to get on the good side of whoever was on duty at the time. It was particularly useful if a client couldn't remember all our names as we said hello or if he was just not fussy and asked the receptionist on duty to recommend a girl. Always good to be fresh in someone's mind.

The bosses were friendly but strict and this was for the good of everyone. A well-ordered house was less stressful. We even had to keep our mobiles in the bathroom in case the ringing annoyed anyone. Either Mr. or Mrs. B would be there, just in case of trouble, and mostly both would be there at night, sitting together watching the telly with us. I don't know how they did it, particularly as the night shift seemed to go on for ever. At least they didn't have to go far—their palatial flat, with a huge snooker table, was directly above us. The only time they weren't there was when they went on holiday for a week every now and then. At those times, either one of the receptionists' husbands or one of Mr. B's huge friends would sit in. We only had trouble twice that I can remember, both occasions at the weekend late at night. One involved a group of drunks who got a little rowdy. They were asked to leave and welcomed back once they had calmed down. The other occasion involved a drunk who couldn't stand up and had to be physically shown out into a cab. Cab drivers were given a fiver for every client that they informed and dropped off our way, so long as the fare stayed for a massage. But this wasn't the best way to gain customers. Repeat satisfied customers made up the bulk of our business; we were very good at that.

A spotless house helped a great deal. Before we came in, invisible cleaners would scrub and vacuum the house from top to bottom. The girls' waiting lounge was a comfortable, snug room with a clean but threadbare carpet. The rest of the house got new carpets and furniture but at the back of the house in the lounge, we made do. It was a little shabby, with three large, odd melamine coffee tables, four old mismatched sofas, and four armchairs, the two on the left for the bosses and the furniture on the right side of the room for us girls.

Mrs. B's office was through a door on the left and the receptionist's desk, chair, and phone were up against the wall by the entrance door. That was the only door used to access the rest of the house. Finally, there was the door to the kitchen, which led through to the laundry and on to the cold, white-tiled bathroom.

I can remember Mrs. B telling me that once you started this type of work, you were hooked; you really don't retire. You take long "holiday breaks" but when you need the money you always come back to it. The scary thing is, I think she might be right!

Mr. and Mrs. B had their spies—they seemed to know everything that went on, no matter how small an incident. Mind you, I don't think they could have missed much, sitting and listening to the chatter and comments that were casually cast out in the girls' lounge. You could learn a lot by just keeping your head down and listening.

It's not that they were listening in to what went on in the rooms, as we rarely spoke to each other about the clients we had just seen. If we did, it was normally to say how pleasant a gentleman had been or to warn other girls, if a particular man had been very rough, to watch out for him in the future. Mr. and Mrs. B had other ways of finding out what went on. On occasion, after you had worked for a couple of weeks, or if they had suspicions, they would send one of Mr. B's close, good-looking friends (the ones we didn't know) to see you in a room and to test your reliability. They would be really nice men and no hassle but would ask you to do things for money that were against the house rules. They would ask you for your number, so they could meet you outside to take you shopping, out for dinner, etc. If you took the bait...took a step out of place, you could be fired soon after. This gave you a really good, true excuse—"How do I know you are not a house trap? I am sorry but I can't take the risk"—to turn down pestering clients who had grown too fond of you and wanted your number, without hurting their feelings and keeping them coming back time and again as regs.

Getting Kitted Out

*O*ur basic uniform for the house was a lacy teddy-type body, easy access with poppers, teamed with hold-ups or stockings and high heels, all in black. With some of the money I had earned, I went shopping for undies to wear for work, as apart from the high heels, I had nothing else suitable in my drawers. Everything I had back then was white and cotton, things I hadn't got round to replacing since I left home. What is it with mothers buying big white pants all the time? It is a myth that G-strings are uncomfortable—it's usually said by women who try squeezing their bottoms into one that's far too small. I, on the other hand, find big pants deeply uncomfortable— almost as bad as a guy with stubble giving you head. Just plain irritating. I had bought a beautiful, expensive black-lace set of underwear once for Patrick, my Boat eye-candy. I was seriously sexually frustrated at the time (no change there then!) and looking forward to picking him up from the station. He was flying in from the States, where he had been on a business trip all that week, and was getting the train down to meet me for a party. On the night, he arrived with a big smile on his face and a pressie for me. He handed over a small black bag, not wrapped in any way. It was some cheap lace black undies, including crotchless panties, a bra, fishnets, and a suspender belt. I acted impressed, but deep down I was a bit disappointed, as I was wearing my lace set. The lingerie he had just handed me was obviously cheap stuff he must have bought from some seedy sex shop. I was not impressed with his taste, but he seemed to like the tacky set better. That was my lesson: expensive undies might turn a girl on but they don't necessarily turn a man on. Sometimes men just like it straightforwardly smutty.

I couldn't for the life of me remember what had happened to those two sets and knew the right underwear was essential for my new job. I found what I needed in a big department store after much traipsing around and trying on various things. I'm not a girl who likes shopping very much (with her own money) and will only shop if I really, really need something, so the task had been a bit of a chore. I knew the exception would be camera-shopping for my Venice trip—going to the shops with my hard-earned cash in my back pocket would be a completely different experience. At least I now knew where to go for my lingerie—the local high street.

So, kitted out in a black-velvet affair with padded lacy cups, I was armed and ready for action for my second shift. I was sitting at the kitchen table, and so far the door had buzzed at least three times and on each occasion someone else had been picked. I'd ducked in the reception room like the others, said my name, and left as quickly as I could as I was still feeling a little nervous.

Not many of the girls were talking to me in the lounge so I sat in the kitchen with a book. Layla nodded to me as she walked in. Being a fellow student, she was friendlier than the rest, making me a cuppa as well as herself. I was stirring my tea when Carry popped her head around the door. I looked up. She nodded to Layla as they passed each other in the doorway.

"Kettle's just boiled," Layla said as she walked out into the lounge.

"Just popped by to pick up a bag I left the other day," Carry said.

I must have looked a bit down because she piped up, "Cheer up, duck." She was going to pass when she stopped at the table and looked at me. "Keep your head down, you're doing OK so far, really. As you're useless at saying hello and no one picks you, the other girls aren't jealous— yet! You look like a kid so bet they are thinking you will only pick up the pervs they don't want—you don't look like competition."

"Right...thank you." I smiled weakly back.

Wonderful. Until then, I had no idea I was a perv magnet!

Despite the weird conversation, at least somebody was speaking to me. I liked Carry's manner, and so asked her something that had been worrying me.

"What do I do if they ask me to do something I don't want to?"

"Tell 'em they can't afford it and laugh it off, humour can get you out of anything. You look so innocent you can get away with acting dumb."

"Gee, thanks, I think..." I had a picture in my head of fending off some big guy coming at me with a rubber chicken with my "humour."

"Honey"—she patted me on the shoulder gently—"they argue less if they think you're daft and don't get the game. Tell 'em it's against house rules if they are being pushy, and failing that leave the room and go to the recep for help. If you can't get out, press the emergency button. That's what it's there for."

"Right, got it," I mumbled, half to myself. "Don't let them get away with things I don't like, act dumb, and be funny, and if all else fails run for it." Sounded like a plan to me!

"Hey, think how uncomfortable you were when you walked in for the first time, that's how they feel," she said, passing into the lounge. "They are far more scared than you are, at least you have them on your home turf—use it to your advantage."

Great—I looked so innocent I was bringing out a sympathetic streak in the older girls and attracting the pervier groups of men. Right, must work on saying hello. Carry left as the buzzer went, whispering, "Say hello more slowly and, for God's sake, smile," and giving me a wink as she walked past me.

I hung back and paid attention to how the other girls said hello. Surprise surprise, the girl who lingered the longest and said hello slooowly got picked. Got it. Look them in the eye and drag it out as long as I can. I did this on the next buzzer. He was mine.

Friday 3rd October

Evening shift 6 p.m.–1 a.m. (although I only lasted until 10 p.m.!)
1 Gemini with Jane (The Doctor) = £15
4 x normal service = £80
Minus £10 receptionist's fee
Total earned: £85

I had five clients on my second shift: a doctor, a pilot, a welder, a holiday-maker, and a student (from a different uni, thank goodness). All had the normal service of the massage and the blow-job, finished off with a fuck, apart from the second client of the evening, the Doctor, who had booked Jane and myself as a Gemini. Jane and I went to the Green Room to massage him together. We had sorted out a plan as we made our way to the room and agreed I would go first and then she would take over to finish him off. A tanned twenty-one-year-old curvy brunette, she worked sporadically to pay her bills, but the whole thing really fucked with her head. She was definitely only doing it for the money and didn't give two stuffs about pleasing her clients or getting repeat business.

Jane chatted away to the client during the massage; I let her lead the way, as she had more experience than me. So, turning him over after the massage to give him head, we took it in turns to suck on each new rubber. I sat on top first, when he was nice and hard, while she leaned over him so he had a face full of her breasts. After much bouncing around on top and his near suffocation under Jane's ample tits we swapped roles. She moved faster, in a rocking motion, while I let him lick my nipples. He eventually came, after much moaning from both of them. It was definitely easier when there were two of you on a guy. Less money was involved, but you didn't have all the responsibility or hassle of dealing with it on your own. It was still strange, as I hadn't really been in that situation with a woman before. The closest I had come was one night with my best mate, Dee, shortly before I was to leave for university. We were at the gym's annual dinner dance. I'd booked a hotel room in the same building and we were in the bathroom together because Dee, who was drunk, had insisted on having a bath before she went home. She's made strange requests when she's had a few too many before, but this was something new! Couldn't talk her out of it, she kept going on about being sticky and was starting to skip to the foyer.

So there we were, Dee in her hot bath and me sitting on the rim looking at my wriggling toes on the damp bath mat. Suddenly, I was pulled backwards into the tub. Dee's arms were wound tightly around me and I now sat on her lap.

Great...I was now soaking wet and there was probably more water on the floor than in the bath! The warm water eased my rawness down below though (too much hanky-panky with Patrick, Mr. Cheap Lace Underwear Boat Boy), which was a plus point, so I stayed put and hugged her back.

"I'm going to miss you, babe," she sniffed as I pulled back. Then she caught me completely unawares by kissing me on the lips. The hand on my breast was a bit of a shock too. I quickly pushed myself out of the bath. "I think I'd better dry off and change," I said, reaching for a towel.

"OK," came the answer from the tub as she happily splashed about, apparently as if nothing out of the ordinary had just taken place.

We never mentioned it again. Weird how the past comes back to give you a hand when you least expect it. I'm not saying the Gemini felt less freaky as a result of Dee, but it all helps!

I carried on the shift, feeling easier about the work as the day went by. All were easy, straightforward guys, mostly in the Mirror Room, which was good in a way as I didn't have to traipse from one room to another, up and down all those stairs, but it was rather disconcerting with all the mirrors, as you could see yourself from all sorts of weird angles. But, having said that, you could also see what a client was up to if he was behind you.

The last client was the student. I was a little swollen by then, and no matter how much I used the K-Y that Layla had given me, it didn't help, especially as the student pounded away for some time before he came. I gritted my teeth till it was over, noticing I was spotting blood when I showered after him. I was glad he hadn't noticed anything; I would have been so embarrassed. In the girls' bathroom, I washed more carefully down below with cold water. I was really bleeding now. The last time had been painful and I couldn't go on any more...I had to stop working. I had a chat with Mrs. B and, thank goodness, she was sympathetic: "Well, you have had a busy day." I had only been on the evening shift but don't think she noticed as I already had five clients down on the clipboard list for payment. She smiled and gave me the number of the local walk-in clinic, explaining that they knew about the sauna and many of the girls went there...you didn't even have to give your name, which was handy.

So I sat in the girls' lounge on a bag of frozen peas wrapped in a tea-towel for some time, listening to Jane passing comments about all guys being twats and picking faults with the guy we had both "Gemini-ed" earlier.

"Stupid bastard tried to stick his fingers up me, so I tried to smother him with my tits...hope he has a sore cock after the fucking he got," she muttered over her coffee. "So your twat of the day was that student?"

"Yep," I nodded. I think Jane really needed to get a grip—she had just come back after quitting a few weeks back. Now she needed rent again, or so she said.

"God, I hate young guys, they must have Duracell batteries in their cocks or something, too much stamina at that age..." On she went with the client-bashing. Layla winked at me and rolled her eyes. All the while I sat there, feeling like faulty goods, waiting for the taxi called by Louise, who was on reception, to take me home. As I left she gave me instructions to call her after I had been to the clinic. That made me feel nervous...I hadn't had the need of a doctor in a long time, and certainly never for such an embarrassing problem, but I hurt so much...I needed professional help and there was no way around it. It wasn't as though I could put a plaster on the cuts or get someone to kiss it better! What a way to end my second shift.

Saturday 4th October: On the Mend

*T*he morning after a really uncomfortable night and the *worst* pain whenever I tried to pee, I put myself in a cab and headed down to the main hospital. The GUM Clinic (Genito-Urinary Medicine, i.e., Sex Clinic, to the rest of the world) was hidden away at the back. I finally found it, after getting extremely lost down long, identical, white corridors. A friendly-looking nurse took my details and gave me a clinic number. Yet another name to add to the rest—what with my new name for work and my classmates giving me a nickname (which I am sooo not going to divulge here), I was amassing a fair few.

It didn't take long before I was seen by a female doctor and nurse. I sat there apprehensively, explaining to them what was wrong. After drawing a curtain around me as I lay on the examination table, they told me to take off my jeans and knickers and lie down. After leaving me to it, they came back when I was ready. I was really nervous and the gentle probing hurt. The doc looked up and said I had a lot of small internal tears and, as I was still so swollen, she could not sew them up. The longer one nearer the entrance was a different matter and seemed to be the cause of most of the bleeding. She could put a dissolvable stitch in it so the bleeding would stop. She said I just needed to relax more while having sex (not another one with a relaxation tip!) and use more lube. Sex would get easier, she promised, but there was not much else she could do. So much for the professionals.

I lay back with my eyes closed, feet in the stirrups, as I was made numb. I tried to think of other things as the small dissolvable stitch was put in place. When I got back to the dorms I took to my bed with a hot-water bottle for the rest of the day and was feeling a hell of a lot better by that evening. I called the sauna the next day to put myself down for another shift the week after just in case. My new doc had said that I should be all right by then—the swelling should be down. But, damn it...my body was not going to let me down. I would have to use the red condoms at work, so the guys wouldn't notice any spots of blood and of course use lots of the K-Y the clinic had given me. There is more than one way to spunk a monkey, isn't there?

I got lots of sleep and did lots of study, stocked up on food supplies when I ventured out, and kept a low profile for the rest of the week as I was still in a bit of pain. I only went to vital classes and held off going into work till I felt better. I tried to hide away from the others in the dorm, too—well, you can't exactly explain internal injuries without giving some background. Luckily, everyone seemed so wrapped up in their newfound freedom they spent most of the time sleeping off their excess behaviour, leaving me free to recuperate in peace and keep telling myself the pain was worth it, that it was all for the good of the Venice fund.

For the first time since I'd started my new job I was able to stop and take stock of the situation. The first week I had been elated, running on a natural high with the excitement...I was still a little naïve at work, as I had only been there a short time, but you learn fast, especially if you do something wrong and it costs you hard-earned cash. In the second week the paranoia had begun to set in: does everyone know? Could people tell? I constantly felt as if eyes were watching me as I walked around—whether I was out shopping, in class, even in my room. Was everyone whispering about me or was I just being oversensitive? As I found out later, this was known in our trade as the "head fuck," it can really mess with your moods. It affects different girls in different ways and can really drag you down unless you stay strong and positive. Weirdly enough, it affects me more the fewer clients I see.

Sunday 12th October

All-day shift 10.30 a.m.–1 a.m.
1 Gemini with Layla = £15
9 x normal service = £180
Minus £20 receptionist's fee, and £10 for Not Keeping My
Mouth Shut
Total earned: £165

Fully healed and back to work, I was still getting used to the gaps between clients—there was still some work I had to do on my kinky hello. But this free time became a godsend for the study I was quite often too tired to think about when I got home after a shift. That Sunday on my third shift was a particularly good day to get uni work done, as I had a couple of classes on the Monday. I wasn't the only student catching up—Layla had her head in an impossibly large medical book that was balanced precariously on her lap. As I sat in the lounge contemplating which textbook to tackle first, I was distracted by a commotion on the main stairs.

Mr. B's two best friends had just won on the races, and the three of them walked in at midday for a drink. I soon learned that one was a chief plumber and the other, a skinny, lanky lad, was his trainee. They had come in via the front and seemed in a very good mood. Mrs. B came over to the lounge from her office and squinted at the small monitor on top of the TV, sighing, but with a smile on her face. "They must have won. Thank god, it's taken long enough!"

They strode into the lounge, as proud as peacocks, and Mr. B went over to his missus, mumbled in her ear, and kissed her cheek.

I kept my head in my book and just listened—so far, I hadn't seen either man walk into the girls' lounge. Everyone else seemed unimpressed, so I decided to play it cool too. I was stretched out on one of the sofas, book in hand, robe firmly belted around me, listening in as the men stood and talked about horses.

"Fine filly with a sleek red coat she was," the plumber was saying to Mrs. B.

"Bit like our new girl then—always knew you were a sucker for a redhead." She nodded in my direction.

He glanced over at me and nodded. "She sure is fine."

So much for fading into the background!

I looked over the top of my book. Suddenly, the chief plumber asked Mr. B if he could take me out to dinner, gesturing in my direction.

I looked at Mrs. B as she shrugged in my direction.

What did that mean? Mr. B looked over to me kindly. "Better ask her yourself."

Deer. Headlights. You get the picture.

Layla still had her head in her book—no help there then.

If there had been a choice, I would rather have gone out with the skinny lad who had gone quiet and been all eyes since he shuffled in, but the other one persisted.

"Hi, I'm Steve, want to go out to dinner some time?" He smiled a gap-toothed grin at me.

Was he a client? Was this a test? I thought I couldn't date clients? Not that I wanted to in this case.

What Carry had said the other morning was still in my head. I had been repeating it as a mantra. Her advice had helped get me picked and had already helped me out of a fix or two with clients who had tried it on, knowing I was new. "Go on, just suck it without," one idiot had begged as he waved a fiver at me. I had giggled, "Sorry, house rules, I can't," and shrugged. Eewww, no rubber? Shudder at the thought.

Carry had given good advice and I tried to think how she would help me out of this new minefield. I lowered my book, looking him square in the face. "You can't afford me, honey." I smiled at him, raised my book, and carried on reading.

Mr. B dissolved into laughter and even Mrs. B tittered away.

"OK, feisty then," Steve huffed. "That showed me!"

Mr. B walked off to the door that led upstairs and ushered Steve and the lanky lad out. I watched them leave and Mr. B winked at me from the doorway.

"We like a girl with guts."

Phew, off the hook. Mrs. B smiled at me and went back to her office as the other girls were still giggling on the sofas.

Layla piped up. "It's OK, Steve's always on the pull!"

"Thanks. You could have warned me!" I stuck out my tongue in her direction.

"Where would be the fun in that?" she grinned back at me.

I also learned to keep my mouth shut on this shift. It was well into the afternoon, and I didn't know when I was sent to a room without saying hello that the guy was a friend of Mrs. B's. I had left him to shower when he told me not to wait, as he knew his way around and was coming up for a chat with Mrs. B after. I got into big trouble when she heard me say to Layla, in passing, that he was the first guy I had only had to give a blow-job to since I had started. So Mrs. B, beckoning me aside, said that, as I had not completed the service for him, I would have to return half the money! She would sort it out. It wasn't my fault he was a touch sensitive! I kept that bit of information to myself, didn't really know what I had done wrong...he had seemed really happy when I left him, grinning from ear to ear. The receptionist gave him back £20. Needless to say, I didn't mention the divorced guy who came in the week after.

A Typical Day in Art

In Studentville, my class was a bit eclectic. Among the eighteen young students, I was classed as a "mature" one. I didn't look "older" (the real definition of mature), but when it is found out you have worked before uni you are automatically classed as mature, rather than just being a student. At least the older lot, if a bit strange, were normally more grounded than the younger gang. They were there because they were sure it was what they wanted to do, it wasn't just something to fill in time and an excuse to have a good piss-up until they decided what they really wanted to do, like the younger lot. The young 'uns, exposed to a life of studentdom, fending for themselves for the first time, quite often went a bit barmy. The freedom was too much. But finding yourself as a person is what being a student is all about, right? Oh, and studying for a good grade, if you have time. When you are an art student, you are told to jump out of the frame and defy convention as soon as you land on campus. I can remember my first lecture, where we were told that "Art is about shocking people." Basically, if you got a reaction—any reaction—the theory was that it was Art.

Well, you can imagine that, after that brief, the class became hell-bent on shocking each other and, more importantly, trying to outdo each other and shock the public. I liked my studies, but increasingly I began to question what it was all about. At least going to work was structured. You knew the rules and where to draw the line. I found uni all a bit topsy-turvy: the reality was that I was going to a brothel in order to escape into sanity/normality. Obviously, a brothel is not "sane," but at least in the workplace you don't walk in and find your work desk screwed to the wall. *You* might be, but at least you are paid handsomely and know where you stand!

The day we arrived in class to find said desk fixed to the wall, I was feeling creative. I arrived early and was glad to find that mine was not the one that had been screwed halfway up the wall. I perched on my stool and started to paint some wide landscapes in mad colours. Painting and drawing have never been my strong point, despite the fact I am good with my hands. Students filtered in and Simon drifted over to see how I was getting on. He lived in halls with me and was the only one I could imagine having anything at all in common with. We had bonded in our first week and I was really starting to like him. As I was settling in at the house, I saw him less and less, despite the fact that he was on the floor below me in the dorm block and we had started to walk to class down the hill together, talking about this and that. Luckily, he didn't seem to have noticed my absence or, if he did, he certainly didn't say.

We talked mostly about art and him and about his partner back home in London. "Up to tricks?" I wished he wouldn't say things like that: it made me very paranoid. All I wanted to say was, "Why, how do you know?" I hadn't told anyone so far about my moonlighting at the bordello so I was a bit anxious.

Did he know? He might be a quiet gay man in his forties and a bit fluffy around the edges as a cover, but I had picked up early on that he was sharp as a tack.

"Darrling, do you have a screw...driver to help poor Natasha get her desk off the wall?" I became convinced that he knew something...but perhaps it was just Simon being Simon?

Simon, Natasha, and I stood on one desk trying to unscrew the other one from the wall. It had to be one of the boys' ideas, probably hoping to look up Natasha's short skirt as she stood on a table.

Natasha was all of nineteen years old, a tall blonde bit of skirt who was pleasant enough, if a bit vague. "Thanks," she purred.

Well, that was it, from now on I would have a shadow in class, as Natasha had twigged that I was quite handy to know. If she couldn't work something out she sidled up to me.

"Think you have a fan," whispered Simon over lunch in the art canteen as Natasha hovered with a tray, coming over and popping herself down next to me, brushing my arm with hers. Great, that's all I needed in my paranoid state. I'd started to live in baggy trousers and outsized jumpers, but just because Simon was gay and I hung around with him didn't make me gay too. Open-minded sure, but unless I was being paid, Princess, these legs stayed closed.

"Hi, Natasha." I smiled politely.

"How's it going? Need any more screwing done?" Simon chirped up.

I kicked him under the table and then stood up to leave them to chat. Natasha grabbed my arm and said she would catch me later. Cute girl, but even if I was into girls, she still wouldn't have been my type. If I liked my boys rough and ready, I suppose my girls would have been the same. Who knows—I am not really that fussy, but chemistry is everything.

Sunday 26th October

All-day shift 10:30 a.m.–1 a.m.
5 x normal service (including Jesse James and Mr. Gay) = £100
1 hour from Jacuzzi = £45
Minus £20 receptionist's fee
Total earned: £125

*M*r. Divorce had problems—the main one being that he didn't want a divorce. He had married five years ago but, from the sound of it, was still living the single life, going out with his friends all the time and working all hours. He was even going away with the boys most weekends—that's how he had ended up here now in the Green Room. He had come in with the lads to have some fun. He seemed urgent and managed to come very quickly...it wasn't my fault. So we talked the rest of the time. He couldn't understand why his wife no longer wanted to sleep with him. She wouldn't talk to him about it, just said she couldn't put up with him any longer.

For me, this job really highlighted the fact that men are really dense sometimes.

"So does she think you're having affair? Or is she just upset she doesn't see you much?" I asked.

"I didn't think of that...might be a bit of both!" he said, genuinely amazed.

He came back a few months later, his marriage back together; she *had* thought he was having an affair, after all! After that he cut back on going out with the lads and spent more time with her. This visit was his first time out with the boys since they had last come in. He had wanted to come back and thank me. All I gave him was a massage as all he did was sit and talk about their relationship...he was being loyal, so he said. I was given a big tip and an even bigger hug before he left. Move over, Carry, you're not the only sex therapist in town.

Mr. Gay was another client on my fourth shift. He was the only other guy I didn't give a proper service to. He came in with a friend one night and the friend was seeing Layla in the room next door. I entered the Parlour to find him fully dressed, seated on the sofa. He didn't want a massage (uh oh, what did he want then? This made me feel uneasy) but he was begging me to stay...it turned out he just wanted me to say he was great in front of his friend, so his mate (who he didn't fancy, he claimed over and over) wouldn't think he was gay and feel uncomfortable around him. Fair enough. He was too scared to tell anyone he was gay and was so desperate I didn't even tell the girls. He stayed the full thirty minutes for good measure and then I showed him up to the reception room, where his friend was waiting impatiently. Showing them out with a big smile, I said I had had a great time and hoped to see him again soon, winking at him. He winked back as I waved them off from the back door. The next day he phoned to tell the receptionist what a great time he had had and how amazing I was. I earned big brownie points from Mrs. B for that—she said I was a good example to the girls! How ironic is that, huh?...The highest recommendation I get is from a man I did nothing with!

It was on this Sunday that I became a little wiser to the ways of the house. Tina was an average-looking girl in her mid-twenties, average height and no real curves. Shoulder-length brown hair. All smiles except when she was hung over—she was a party girl and the house snitch. Mrs. B paid her on the quiet for information—in fact, I think she earned more this way as she got far fewer clients than most of the girls, so I suppose it was her way of upping her money. A smile goes a long way in getting you clients, but it won't keep them if you're a lousy lay.

Most of the girls didn't bother with new girls till they knew they were going to stick it for at least a week, and with some it would be a couple of weeks before they would even speak to you. That in itself would often scare off the timid. There really is no room in a whorehouse for a timid whore, as they take more looking after and pampering than a dependent gimp, which isn't handy. It's just really annoying when they get in the way. Tina wasn't like that, but she had a different agenda, which wasn't altogether clear at this point.

Tina had at least been friendly to me, even though I hadn't been there long, having made me at least two cups of tea and chatted about this and that. She was friendly to everyone so no one thought much of it. Only a few of the girls of long-standing knew what was really going on, I realized, but they kept quiet about her being the house snitch and Mrs. B's best source.

As I was saying hello that morning, first in line, I had noticed a ladder starting in the toe of my stocking. I took my shoes off in the lounge and padded into the kitchen on my way to the bathroom, pulling off the offending stocking. The ladder had just raced up my leg, so was well past fixing with a dab of clear nail varnish. I was doubled over to look at the ladder when I heard the hushed voices of Tina and Mrs. B. They couldn't see me, because I happened to be in the doorway just behind the freezer. I had thought Tina was busy with a client, as she hadn't been in the line to say hello with the rest of us. The house liked as many girls as possible to say hello, as it gave a good impression. Even if a girl had just come up from a room and hadn't had time to drop her rubbish bag in the bin or tidy up, she could still get grabbed on her way through to say a quick hi, even if there were already a few girls in line. You might even have to say hi twice in the hope that the client was so bewildered he wouldn't notice you making up numbers. Now I realized that Tina wasn't with a client. Hushed voices just make you strain to listen—it's human nature—so I kept as still as I could.

"Cebell says Jane just called in—she's just come on," mumbled Mrs. B.

"No, she was with us last night on the lash, so she's probably hung over. She had her period last week and was blocking," Tina whispered back. The easiest way still to have sex when on your period is to block, and I was taught this by Carry. I have seen many things used in the past, even a ball of cotton wool soaked in K-Y. This can tend to disintegrate, though, and be hard to feel to pull out. Clinics used to provide contraceptive-disk sponges that you would use hygienically to block the flow, so you could still have sex. But they did not work well as a contraceptive device and the local health authorities stopped supplying them. That was when ladies had to get creative.

Some girls use a diaphragm to block, but it can be uncomfortable working, with all the movement and different positions. Latex-only foam sponges (as they hold together better when you pull them out) cut into a rectangle one inch by two worked for me. It's softer, and men can never feel it in you. You have to boil the sponge first, soak in K-Y to make it softer and hook it out with two fingers in a tweezer-like motion straight after. It can't get lost up there, can't go too far, as the opening to your womb is too small to let it in. When wet and heavy, gravity will help it out or, if you can contract your muscles, you can sometimes push it out. Blocking saves you from missing a shift and having to take time off. It makes you a more valued girl to the house and the bosses as they know at least you will be turning up reliably to work.

I knew I was too close to them to stay hidden, so I backed out and walked straight back into the main part of the kitchen.

"Tea?" asked Tina, standing by the sink.

"Yep, please," I said with a smile, walking through to change my stocking. What was it my gran kept on saying?

"Keep your friends close and your enemies closer." Keeping my ears open the way I do, I probably would have gathered what was going on given a couple of months. Jane got a late-call cancellation fee added against her name on the chart for her next shift, which covers the cost of getting another girl to come in on short notice, known as sick-shift cover.

If you let the house know in time, you avoid being fined, but if you phoned in at the last minute you would have to pay a fine, the only exception being if you had just come on your period and didn't block. A period was the most common reason for calling in a sick day and you would be rotated and not lose a work day. Not calling in or having a hangover was not a reason. And Jane paid the price.

A lot of the girls didn't ever really know the score about Tina, even after a couple of months, so it was lucky that I had an early warning. I made a mental note not to tell Tina anything I didn't want Mrs. B to know. Another life lesson: be careful what the hell you say, even to people you think are your friends. In a way, keeping quiet about Tina being a snitch meant that the girls who were up to no good and who could endanger your position were weeded out. In total, I reckon only one in ten girls who worked there knew about Tina, the others just thought Mrs. B had eyes in the back of her head.

As I kept a low profile and never did much untoward, they had no reason to snoop on me. I just made sure that I didn't say a word to anyone if I had a client who a) came before I went near him, b) just had a blow-job, c) just wanted a massage and nothing else, or d) just wanted to chat: I certainly didn't want to be made to give any of my money back. I handed in most tips, but if I was having a good bouncy day and lots of guys were tipping me or if I got one big tip, I made sure I only handed half of it into the recep for safe-keeping, as the last thing I needed was for anyone to assume that a big tip equalled me doing extras! For the record, extras normally include kissing, oral without a condom, anal, or rimming (licking a guy's ass or having yours licked out), or basically anything else the other girls wouldn't do. I didn't do extras, not because I was sniffy about it, I just didn't need to—the job was difficult enough as it was. You get the basic massage and a suck followed by a fuck, both with a rubber, and that's it, your time's up, honey. If I had wanted to do other things I would have worked somewhere else...and been better paid.

Extras were, most of the time, the territory of desperate girls who needed the cash—girls like Suzie, our amateur porn star in her late twenties. She didn't have a particularly good figure at all and had deflated, saggy, post-kid tits. She was saving up for a boob job. She was sneaky, manipulative, and always looking for a way to make an extra buck, just like Paris (another nightmare), but unlike Paris, she wouldn't tell you straight to your face. Suzie wouldn't hesitate to sneak around saying she was your best friend while stabbing you in the back when you least expected it. With her lank brown hair and uneven complexion covered in make-up, she was the girl who any guy went to for back-door business. I'm not sure how much extra she charged, but Mrs. B tended to overlook any of Suzie's dealings as long as she kept it quiet. Suzie never handed in any tips at all and got away with it. After all, a porn star working for the house was good for business—guys went all boggle-eyed at the mere mention of it most of the time.

Other girls giving extras were normally fired, although you never knew for sure as they just disappeared. So, unless you were doing badly, really needed the money, and were willing to risk your health, it was never worth it. All this meant that getting heavy tips was not necessarily a good thing for your reputation. On the other hand, if you didn't give in some of your tips (you got them back at the end of the shift with your other money), it looked as if you were crap at your job. Guys tip good girls, mostly a fiver. Up to £20 had been known, but that was rare.

Obviously, the top girls had more leeway with the bosses—you could get away with a bit more and got the choice shifts. They wanted to keep you and keep you happy as a top earner, making them money in turn. They noted the tips, and this helped in calculating your status, along with how many regulars came in to see you, how many last-minute sick-cover shifts you did, and how punc-tual you were. Clients calling in asking for you or who asked when you were next working always pleased Mrs. B too. When I found that out, if a guy asked when I was next working while I was showing him out, I started to say "I think such and such a day...but you might just want to call and check first." I even went so far as handing out house business cards with the phone number. Sneaky? You bet. But it kept me on top, and that is a position this girl is quite fond of.

Back to Uni...

*B*y the fourth week I had become slightly agoraphobic. I didn't go out much and, if I did, it was at night. I kept my head down and studied...It distracted me from my paranoia. Also, I had started to dress more soberly when out and about so as not to be noticed—baggy clothing, trousers, and trainers helped me to feel less obvious, but there was still the "smell" theory. That's what us girls put it down to, that men must subconsciously know when you are sexually active, because they just start to come out of the woodwork. I must have been sending out pheromones or something, I felt like I couldn't go out without being pestered by some man or other, and it's not as if I was wearing anything provocative or they had recognized me from the house. I was really anxious about being followed around by some weirdo who wouldn't take no for an answer. It had happened a few times already, so I put off phoning in for another shift till I really needed the money and until I checked the balance of the camera fund and started to panic that I might not be able to afford the trip.

There was a guy in my dorm block called Ethan, who seemed at first to be immune to my pheromones. He'd been the first person I met when I arrived at university. Tall, dark, a bit podgy, but still a fairly good-looking twenty-seven-year-old. "I want me some of that" was my first thought when I spotted him. He was in his last year and was a sort of caretaker for the whole block. The girls were on the ground two floors and the boys on the top two. We were an extremely mixed group in age, colour, and nationality—most of the foreign students were housed here. I had arrived two days early, before any other student, in order to get a good room and had managed to score one in the newest block. They normally reserved this nice block for the foreign students. It was some way from the main campus, but at least it was near the centre of town and my art department was only a few roads away, so it was very convenient for me. It cost a bit more than the standard rooms, but it was perfect.

The floors were split into two blocks made up of five bedrooms, all en suite, with a communal kitchen. I happened to be on a floor with four mad Swedish girls all studying business and tourism. They were fun, but a bit of a handful. The whole block was really sociable. I would stop and chat to Ethan in the corridor and a group of us would sometimes spend the evenings together playing cards. On Sundays, ten of us would get together on the top floor. Ethan and a few others would cook Sunday lunch; it helped to stop some of the other students feeling homesick.

However, I soon started drifting away from the student group of friends I had come to know in the block. What with the studying, classes, and work, I was just never around to chat and couldn't attend the Sunday lunches any more, as I had started doing the all-day Sunday shifts at work. I would get back late and explain away my late-night activity as work at a local casino to anyone who asked. Ethan saw straight through me, however, so I told him where I was working. He was OK about it, just told me to be careful.

I would pop my head round Ethan's door if his light was on when I came back from a shift, mostly just to chat, if he was alone. If he wasn't, I would head on up to my room. It was getting more and more difficult to explain where I had been at that time of night, as everything was shut that late and sometimes I didn't get back till 3 a.m. or later...it was suspicious, to say the least.

I was getting on well with Ethan. A few of the other girls flirted with him, but I didn't see him respond. It seemed that the path was clear...or so I thought. By way of a note under his door, I invited Ethan up to my room at eight one Wednesday night. Strangely enough, I have never been the best at chatting up a bloke. It helps me when it's the other way around and I am being pursued. You would think all my sexual experience would help, but when you're paid for your couchie the flirting part gets stifled—believe it or not, I am totally pants at it!

Ethan knocked on my door promptly at eight and came in. After many flirting attempts on my part, I simply jumped on him...I couldn't wait. On the bed with his pants and trousers down around his ankles, he lay back looking very relaxed, his hands behind his head. Cocky bastard.

Rounding on him with a rubber, I did what I do best, but he came prematurely. It was a bit of a blow, as I had hoped for a long romp that would last all evening. Bounding off the bed, he pulled his pants back on, thanking me as he started to head out the door, all the while saying, "Sorry to shoot and run" (yeah, yeah, very funny), but he was meeting Julie down the hall, they were going for dinner. "I *did* know he was dating her, didn't I?" Well, apparently everyone else did! I sat on the bed, left totally bemused as he sauntered out of my room. Bloody news to me...I hadn't heard a thing about Julie! My playmate situation had changed beyond all recognition. I think Ethan avoided me after that, which was fine by me as I had gone right off him. I started to think about leaving the dorm and asked around if anyone had a room for rent.

In fact, by then everything had really started to fuck with my mind, and one evening it was all brought to a head. Harry, on the next floor of our dorm block, had a big epileptic fit. He'd told me about his epilepsy one day but reckoned he could keep his fits under control. He was a tubby, cute, dark-haired boy doing law and had only gone and had a fit in the middle of the night. His next-door room mate, Sebastian, had a spare key for Harry's room for emergencies—just as well, as he heard loud banging on his friend's wall in the night. He let himself in and tended to Harry, wrapping his bleeding head in a towel. After grabbing someone to sit with the nearly unconscious Harry, he then went looking for me. Somehow, he had remembered a fleeting conversation over a Sunday lunch in which I had said I was qualified in first aid. Harry was quite dopey at that point and the bunch of eighteen-year-olds didn't know what to do and were panicking as it became obvious that he had lost a lot of blood. It looked a hell of a lot worse than it actually was. They couldn't find me, of course, as I was at the house, working. I doubt I could have done much, but they were desperate and then started to worry about where the hell I was, given it was gone 3 a.m. Everything was closed and even the hardiest of clubbers were tucked up in their beds by then. I came back just as the ambulance pulled up. A crowd had gathered, everyone in their PJs standing quietly in the cold. I thought it was a fire alarm at first—that wouldn't have been so bad as I could have snuck back into the crowd—but then I saw a bloody Harry being stretchered off. I approached the block in my coat and jeans across the empty car park, only to be greeted by lots of awkward questions. Where the hell had I been? Bloody hell, it was getting really difficult to sneak off. I cobbled something together about working as a waitress at an illegal gambling den. Oh, what a tangled web we weave...

Bugger, it's hard to keep things straight when you have to lie to everyone all the time. So many nosy students, so many nosy questions. It was just a pain, I wasn't used to lying to cover my ass—it wasn't second nature to me then. This episode was definitely a major catalyst for me moving on. I thought that I would feel more comfortable living somewhere more discreet.

I was helped in my search for new accommodation by Layla. Mrs. B told her I was looking for a place and I stepped up the search after the Harry fiasco. Layla and her flatmate had a spare room. Handy! Female flatmates who knew what I did, didn't care, and didn't need to ask questions because they already knew. No more lying.

My mind was made up: my coming and going at all hours was starting to provoke far too many questions in the dorm, and my answers just weren't convincing enough. The situation was making me uncomfortable, particularly as Julie was starting to become friendly with me and I didn't have the heart to tell her what a player her new boyfriend Ethan was...she seemed so happy and I didn't want to interfere. The Ethan episode put me off dating or playing around for quite some time. I couldn't believe I had been so dense. Fact was I had all the sex I needed anyway and, with my days being so busy, I didn't miss the dating scene or feel the need to find new playmates, not for now anyway.

Moving On

So that's how I came to be living down the road with Layla and Sanita. I went over there one afternoon to check their flat and we sat around drinking tea. We all got on so well that I decided to move there and then. It took me a few days to move my stuff over, as I didn't have a car at that point (camera and Venice came first, after bills and rent!) and had to carry everything in boxes to my new room. I decided not to take a shift at the house while I moved and settled in, as I still had my studies to cope with as well and didn't want to fall behind. I had enough saved up for a deposit and rent, as I had spent hardly any of the money I'd worked so hard for (I had roughly £400 tucked away in the bank after only four shifts). Let's just say the area wasn't very inspiring and everything was quite cheap. After £40 on rent/bills a week and about the same on food— I am not a big partier or clothes shopper even now—it was hard to spend over £100 in a week. I know that sounds stupid for a student, but I didn't spend like one. I didn't smoke, buy music, drink, take drugs, or whatever else students usually spend money on. My mother taught me how to budget properly, so I saved. I know, I know, I sound like a Stepford Wife and, yes, before you ask, I can bake too.

I got on really well with Layla, and this was helped by the fact that she was at the same uni as me. Layla's family were originally from Oman. Dark-skinned with beautiful, long dark hair, she was all curves, and rather busty. She was working to put herself through university to be a doctor. Sanita, with whom she shared the large flat, was another working girl. I didn't know her so well as she worked different shifts. She was sweet but barely around most of the time so, despite living together, we really didn't see that much of each other. She was a Chinese girl in her late twenties, shorter than me, with short bobbed hair and a smidgen overweight. She was fairly shy and kept to herself.

It was the middle of November when the first row occurred. Layla stormed in, throwing her bag down. She was fuming. I had not been living at the flat for very long and hadn't yet seen her lose her rag.

A comment shouted from a car window, telling her to go back to where she came from, had enraged her. She had been born in this country and spoke perfect English so "how dare they" judge her just by the way she looked!

"Take a deep breath and have a cup of tea, I've just boiled the kettle," I voiced sympathetically from the sofa. Tea solves almost anything. But obviously not today it didn't. It became clear that that had been the wrong thing to say. She erupted.

"How would you know—being white—what it feels like to be picked on because of your colour? Teased at school— called names—how could you possibly know?"

Well, I wasn't going to take that sitting down! So, following her into the kitchen, I shouted my opinion straight back at her. This was one of the very few times in my life that I have ever really shouted at anyone, and I let her have it both barrels.

"I don't know what it feels like to be picked on because of colour?" I was indignantly pointing at my head with both hands. "Have you seen my hair lately? I'm a bloody Belisha beacon! How many kids at your school were your colour?"

"Forty," she replied calmly, stopped in her tracks, looking back at me. (Trust me: I may be little but if I shout you can hear me miles off.)

I was just getting going. "Well, there were three of us redheads in a school of five hundred! And you don't think I was bullied—held by the throat, pinned up against the wall in the girls' loos, my hair pulled out in clumps, my homework stolen out of my bag and made into confetti! 'Ginger,' 'carrot-top!'"—I took a breath—"just because *my hair was a different colour!*" I took an even deeper breath to try and calm down.

She stumbled over her words. "I'm sooo sorry...I didn't know...Can't believe I judged you like that, babe, I feel such a hypocrite." She was visibly shocked at my outpouring and our shouting match was over as soon as it had started. We sat, we had tea...it was the British thing to do.

I know it sounds stupid now, but I hadn't really thought of Layla or Sanita as being a different colour up to then. Thinking about it now, I have a lot of friends of all different colours, shapes, sizes, and orientations. It never occurred to me before, don't see why it should. I think I'm pretty open-minded (I would hope so, given the life I have led). I was a bit taken aback two weeks later when Sanita appeared in the living room in full silk Chinese dress—a dark green top, side slit, with matching trousers. She looked stunning. She was off, she explained, to visit her parents; there was an important family gathering, hence the get-up. She really hated formal dress and much preferred her jeans, trainers, and sweatshirts. She didn't talk much about her family, only that she didn't like them very much as they had wanted her to marry someone and had turned her out on the street when she refused. A quiet, calm person, she would come back looking washed out and sullen after family visits. They were rare, to say the least, but out of some weird sense of duty she was trying to make peace with them.

There was never any jealousy or bitchiness over clients as we were all so different. What with seeing as little of each other as we did, due to the fact we often worked different shifts, had different classes, and different friends, we got on really well. Layla and I spent more time together on the whole, as we often both worked the Sunday shift. Sanita preferred the Saturday, as it was busier. She also went to a different uni, a language school down the road, so we hardly saw her during the week, let alone at weekends. Our flat had two rules which we all mutually consented to: no smoking in the lounge and no men in the flat...not even male friends. A bit tricky if you were dating a guy but, quite frankly, we never had the energy to date much as well as work. Too many questions and too many problems. Who needed the hassle!

Tuesday 18th November

Evening shift 6:30 p.m.–1 a.m.
3 x normal service (including Young Runner For England—way too
nervous; Old Human Resources Guy—£7 tip; and the Chinese) = £67
1 hour (with Mark the Bouncer with the Dragon Tattoo) = £40
1 hour from Jacuzzi (with John, who came in late) = £45
Minus £10 receptionist's fee
Total earned: £142

I was happy with the way my life was going so far. I was feeling more settled, and work at the house was fitting in with my studies really well. Sod's Law, though, that just when everything's going nicely, life reverts back into a bitch and bites you on the bum. Something nasty was bound to happen—and it did.

On my first shift after having moved into my new accommodation I was selected by the Chinese man I saw on my first day. We made our way to the Velvet Room. This time he acted slightly differently. He pinned me down the same as before and held both my hands firmly above my head with one of his hands. He then entered me. I struggled to free a hand up so that I could hold the condom that I had put on him, but it was over so fast. He came, and I only really noticed the rubber was not on as I sat up. I couldn't reach the panic button in that position even if I had wanted to. I think I was in shock—everything was happening in slow motion. He was dressing quickly, without having had a shower. I picked the empty rubber off the floor with a tissue, collected the rubbish, and showed him to the door like some kind of zombie.

Back in the girls' lounge, I was in a daze as I explained what had happened. Mr. B bolted for the door, swearing under his breath as Tina put her arm around me and took me to the loos. The guy had gone. Mr. B is a big bloke and if he had caught the Chinese guy I know that I wouldn't have been the only one visiting the hospital. Why hadn't I pressed the alarm? Shouted out? It was over so quickly that I could not think of what had happened. Had I been raped? "He didn't seem bothered about it at all," I wittered away to Tina.

"Did he take it off? Or did it fall off?" she pressed. Quite possible—after all, he was rather small! I was too confused. I just shrugged. Nothing could be done now to change what had happened...the deed was done.

"Do you want to go home?" Tina asked. "Louise will order you a cab..."

It seemed as if they all thought I should go, but I was adamant: I wanted to stay till the end of the shift. All I wanted was a shower, then I would be fine. One of the girls in the bathroom told me not to shower up myself, as it could wash anything that was there further up, but just scoop it out with my fingers wrapped in an inside-out condom. Maybe the spermicide would help.

Getting pregnant was not what was worrying me—I was still on the pill because of my irregular periods, had been since I was twelve—it was all the sexual infections I could catch that worried me. I had some tests done at the clinic. The wait for the results was awful—the longest three months of my life! I carried on working, because the damage had been done and I might need the money for the future. I tried hard to push it all to the back of my mind. From then on I was a girl on top and in charge! I put the sum of money I had so far saved into a new fund for a car or just in case. (This was extra, as I had earned enough for the Venice fund. The camera was bought.) Finally, the results came back: I was fine. Life could carry on as normal. Even though I'd had a scare, I didn't feel it was the house's fault. I still felt safe there. It certainly wasn't going to stop me, not now. During my time in the house, I saw lots of Chinese clients, who were sooo much nicer than the first one. I was popular with them as I am so petite they didn't find me intimidating, and when they find a girl they like, they recommend her to all their friends! I was infamous at the local Chinese restaurant—in the end, all the male staff came to the house, separately, during my time there: waiters, chefs, the master chef, and even the manager! I didn't dare go in there, but I probably could have had a free meal or two had I needed it!

The whole thing felt secure, in general. At least I wasn't getting blind drunk like the rest of the student girls in the dorms and going off with strangers, waking up in strange places, not knowing where they were or how they got there! Hell, I could have just as much fun. I didn't need to get plastered to lose my inhibitions—and I got paid! The irony is that me and my fellow girls get tarred with the cheap-slut/whore brush while there are people out there who do it for free and take huge risks. As I don't have too many hang-ups in the first place, I don't have to glug on the end of a bottle of alcopop to get my party started. I'm lucky that way, I suppose. Mind you, maybe it would help if I had more inhibitions—maybe.

The most annoying question that would crop up when chatting with clients was, "Does your family know what you do?"

"Does your wife know that you're here?" I would counter, puzzled at the point of the question. It was hard enough trying to convince my mother that just because I hadn't had a boyfriend or a date for a couple of years, it didn't mean I was a lesbian. Talk about jumping to conclusions! Despite this sticking point, I have the coolest mother in the world—it was official as a kid that Mum was the mum everyone wanted as theirs. They still do, although she would never believe it. She brought us up to be strong, smart, independent women. I still feel very guilty when she says things like, "I can't have been a bad mum to bring up two perfect girls," closely followed by the sentence that always makes me cringe: "Your sister might be bossy and you're obstinate, but at least you two are sensible and not standing working on street corners or shooting up drugs." My mum thinks the worst thing that could happen to a person would be to become a junkie street-walker. (I have seen worse, but have no inclination to inform her about this.) I have heard the standing-on-street-corners speech five times since I started my adventure in the sexual underworld.

From the impressions given by the media, I can just imagine what the average person who has never been inside a brothel would think of a house. I, too, had preconceived ideas, fostered by what I had seen and read. I know that Mum would understand in the end, if I had a long talk with her, but she is a worrier and has a tendency to panic a little in most situations and I have no intention of worrying her or anyone else in my family if it's not necessary.

I was trying hard not to go home too much any more. I was enjoying my new life and the freedom it brought—it was one big clandestine adventure. I love my family to death, but they can be draining. I have always felt like the family's shrink, especially when living at home. If my parents fought and had been shouting at each other, they would come separately to me afterwards. It was all so stressful; I hated the fights, the screaming fits, the shouting. I can't stand stress, it's not in my nature. I can stand up for myself, but I used to shut myself in my room till the storm blew over...it was taken for grumpiness but it was self-preservation. Like pretty much every family, when you go back to visit they drive you potty. I covered up my job by saying that I worked in a call centre at night and they couldn't call me as I wasn't allowed my phone on the job. It was the only way to explain all the nights they couldn't get hold of me.

Falling into a routine was becoming easier. The house was comfortable and homely. My shifts were always filled with different people and experiences, sex had become much easier and playing around, dressing up when I was in the mood, was fun. We did have outfit changes every now and again. When regulars requested a uniform change, we had a rack of flimsy things in the girls' changing room. Oh la la...all the French Maid outfit really consisted of was a see-through black net dress, off the shoulder, short-sleeved, short-skirted, trimmed with the obligatory white lace with a lace apron sewn on. You couldn't really wear your bra with it and guys would find no knickers...very naughty. If you were feeling playful you took the feather duster with you. It was very popular, that outfit, and I would parade around the designated room, a set of eyes following me as I bent over and dusted things, ass in the air so he would have a good view of the tops of my stockings and bottom, stopping in front of him to dust him, as if he were part of the room.

Sukey was very popular in that outfit, even though she hated it. It really suited her with her long, straight black hair. She was in her early twenties, slim, fit, over-tanned, small-chested, and wore lots of gold chains. A strong accent from the local council estate didn't help and her strong personality could scare some clients off. She had been a teenage mother on an estate, which probably explained her hardened attitude. She had to fight hard to care for her child.

The Jungle Jane outfit was scraps of animal-print silky nylon, the bottom part consisting of a slashed, gathered short skirt and the top part a boob tube made of the same stretchy fabric. My black stockings looked a little strange when paired with the ensemble, but I needed an easy hiding place for the obligatory rubber, a safe, undisturbed place, as I disrobed and pounced wildly on my unsuspecting prey.

The Head Mistress cape was mostly worn by either Bella or Kerry. Off they would totter to a room, a mortar board on their head, a curved-handled cane in hand. A swishing noise always preceded a punctuated yelp from the Ballroom when it was Bella. I really think she liked that get-up more than she let on. I, on the other hand, couldn't be persuaded.

Tuesday 25th November

Evening shift 6:30 p.m.–1 a.m.
5 x normal service = £100
Minus £10 receptionist's fee
Total earned: £90

I started to gain my own regulars pretty fast. Among them was my calm and steady rock, Blessed Brian, a middle-aged man, a bit portly and with thinning red hair, who would be in to see me every Sunday morning without fail, except if he was on holiday or at work. An easygoing, no-fuss, predictable kinda guy. I knew what I was getting—a short sharp screw. What a lovely way to warm up on a Sunday. He never talked about anything personal, so I have no idea what he did for a living, he was just a nice guy. When I eventually left the house, Brian was there on my last shift, which just happened to be on a Sunday. I had told him I was leaving the week before, so on my last day he had wished me luck, given me a box of chocolates (which I shared with the girls) and a bottle of the perfume

I liked at the time. After hugging me and waving goodbye, he sauntered off out the back door.

But as well as the easy clients there inevitably came the chore of dealing with the real nightmares. Mr. Drunk ("Do you like my body...I'm hot, aren't I?"), Gary, the twat, would stumble in very late in the evenings asking to see me. He was the archetypal drunk man who would jerk you around. A pussycat when sober and just plain annoying when he'd had too much booze. If a massage made him doze off it was difficult to rouse him. If he wasn't sleepy, he would be talking nineteen to the dozen about nothing in particular; he was all talk and no trousers, with a Yo-Yo dick. I would spend ages sucking him to get it up, only to be foiled when, stopping to reposition myself, he would deflate yet again. Disheartened and frustrated, I would have to start over...and all the while he would be complaining: "God, this is weird, it never happens when I have a drink normally!..."

Really—alcohol being a dick depressant, what are the odds of that?

He was the winner in the droopy-dick category if ever I met one. Dealing with him in that state was tiring and potentially painful, as he tended to be too heavy-handed trying to "excite" me. The knock on the door letting me know that my time was up never came soon enough, and his predictable parting shot was always the same: "You enjoyed that so much *you* should be paying *me*."

I hated it when they said that. It's a standard punter line uttered by men who think they are studs but are in reality insecure little boys who are so crap in bed that you have to overact and fake it with so much heavy breathing that your mouth feels like the Gobi Desert by the end of the session. Pay *him*! Yeah, right, I thought as I smiled and waved him out. He wasn't the one who would have fingerprint bruises the next day from all the mauling! His type were worst at the weekends, when they would bundle into the house in packs feeling horny. If you could put up with all the hassle on a Friday- and Saturday-night shift, it was a good little earner, but extremely knackering.

Talking about extremely knackering shifts, a tallish man in smart suit, sharp tie, and a curly moustache was another regular. "Arab Ali" is what he called himself. He mostly came in at the end of the month for his pay-day treat. A bit of hassle with over-familiar hands (code for if you're not into anal, keep an eye on his fingers) by then wasn't anything I couldn't handle—he was just extremely draining because he was so opinionated. He loved a Gemini, and Layla was his other favourite, so if we happened to be on the same shift he was one happy man. We were a very striking pair, her dark to my light. Her smooth, large assets in comparison to my small tits were a wonderful sight. One of us would always be picked, no matter which other girls were there. As time went on, Layla and I were stopped from working too many shifts together, as the other girls wouldn't earn much on those days, and that did not make for a happy house.

He liked a long massage and would adore it if Layla walked over his back. I would stand there at the side of the bed to hold her steady; it wasn't an easy thing to do on a sprung mattress. After the massage we took it in turns to give him head. First one of us would sit on top while the other let him suck her tits, then we would swap. Whoever was on top at the end was in charge of ensuring his climax.

Just to be clear, lesbian "Shows" were...well...different from a Gemini. Layla didn't really go in for shows, so when I eventually plucked up the courage I was paired off with Samantha. I loved doing a show with Samantha, she was so much fun. She was an ex-body-builder in her early thirties; blonde, fit, and feisty, she was saving for a house after the end of an abusive relationship. We were a bit of a handful together, both fit and energetic. As we stripped and sucked each other's nipples then ventured further down, the guy was normally mesmerized, settling into a better position as we got into a 69 ready for the next stage. Getting out the double-ended dildo while on all fours, we would suck on a rubber that covered each end, sucking and licking each end of the phallus, and culminate in a kiss. Having applied lots of lube, we would get on to our backs. Cheek to cheek, legs bent up, we would insert the hard end, moving it back and forth. If the guy watching wasn't masturbating, we would get him to hold the dildo in the middle. This was so we could roll over on all fours and back on to each end for better penetration. If one of us kept still and in the same position, we would have an excited penis to suck as well, leaving the other girl to carry on. In that situation, the poor guy never knew which one of us girls to pleasure first—he definitely had his hands full! In the end we were lucky girls indeed if he didn't shoot his load before we got to try him out.

Although I obviously do like men, in a weird way, I like women too. I went through a stage where I even dated a woman for a while, a few years after leaving the house. I went back to men in the end, though; I missed the power of all that testosterone and of a satisfying member.

In this job, you have to be very skilled at understanding men and, on the whole, I could spot a liar a mile off, for example, The Man with Shiny Shoes, a client who claimed to be an astronaut for NASA (a pilot from the nearby airbase would have been more likely). It was his shiny shoes that gave him away as a copper, and only a copper would have really known what was in the locker room at the local police station.

He happily informed me that the local police bulletin board had an interesting notice to the effect that we were the only house in the area which all officers (if they have to use a sauna) were allowed to use, as we were the only house considered safe and clean. Talk about a recommendation! You can normally spot a copper straight off: they make the worst liars—always too much information and always tripping themselves up with inconsistencies. Anyhow...news of this notice reached the ears of Mr. B, who duly informed us that it was indeed true. How he knew it was true we didn't like to ask. I don't think Mr. B was ever in the police, it was more likely that one of the old cronies he played cards with was a top copper. Despite my unfamiliarity with the police force, I was soon to have my hands full dealing with a real policeman.

Sunday 30th November: The Police Raid

7 x normal service* = £140
Minus £10 receptionist's fee
Total earned: £130
*non police

*I*t was early in the afternoon when we were raided by the police. We saw them piling in on the cameras, more than twenty of them; we later found out that a girl who was fired for taking drugs in the house had a police officer as a client and had happily taken her revenge for losing her job by telling him a heap of lies to get the house into trouble.

We panicked as soon as we saw the uniforms on camera, and Kerry and I bolted through a private entrance upstairs to Mr. and Mrs. B's flat. The Bosses were nowhere to be seen. I wondered later if they'd had a tip-off, as their absence that day was very unusual. Mr. B would usually have been sat back in his chair by now reading the Sunday papers, having popped out for a stroll in the morning. Sitting in the kitchen, Kerry and I pretended we were having tea and chatted as calmly as we could, holding our cups, perched on the kitchen stools in our dressing gowns. We hoped that being in a different building, technically with a different address, would help to distance us from the raid. We were wrong—they knew exactly where to find us.

A couple of minutes later two officers burst into the flat and asked if there was anyone else up there, before escorting us back down to the girls' lounge. We still had no idea what was going on. The girls huddled in a group by the window and Cebell was gesturing madly, demanding to know what was going on. They'd had a tip-off, we were told, that we were all using drugs! So they were here to search the premises. Thank god! It was a huge relief to know that we weren't going to be thrown into the back of a van, although we were a bit apprehensive, as there was always the worry that one of the new girls might have something stashed in her bag.

Frog-marching us one at a time to the bathroom, our bags were searched and our coat pockets turned out. A pompous, plain-looking man with a really patronizing way about him looked down at me and demanded my name and address. I gave a false one; after all, it was against house rules to give out your real details. I had seen many policemen come in for a massage (amusingly, their requests were some of the stranger ones we received), but whoever was asking, I didn't want anyone knowing where I lived. It made me feel uneasy, even if it was a police officer. But, he soon found out the truth after searching my bag. All the info he needed was in the letter from the student-loans department I'd received that morning. I had been returning my loan and still had all the paperwork with me. He raised an eyebrow, scratched out my previous details, then wrote in the correct ones he now had in front of him.

"Do you have any drugs in here?" he grunted, picking up my bag and tipping the rest of the contents on to the floor while I watched.

"No," I said.

He proceeded to put back the items one at a time, with a gloved hand, as if he would catch something.

"You must really hate men to work here," he muttered under his breath.

"I love men actually—that's *why* I work here."

He glared at me after that. Checking my coat pockets, he told me to go with the female officer who had just strode in.

I was ushered into the Yellow Room by two female officers and told they were going to strip-search me to see if I had any drugs. Feeling apprehensive and with as much dignity as I could muster, I started to strip off, handing each item to the tall, pale brunette who was standing at the foot of the bed, close to the door. She checked each item I gave her. When naked, the two women just stared at me.

"You are not touching me unless you change your gloves, I don't know where they have been," I informed them, and with that I lay on the bed and spread my legs in the air. They both turned red, mortified; I don't think they were expecting that. I reiterated that I had nothing to hide. They didn't touch me, just looked away, horrified, and told me to get dressed. It was OK, I could go, they had only wanted to check my clothing! That made me smile.

Talking with the wide-eyed girls back in the lounge, I told them what had happened when I stripped. The consensus of the small group was that it served them right for looking down their noses at us.

No drugs were found that afternoon. They probably would have had better luck if they had raided the bank down the road, where a bank-manager client of mine had proudly told me that he kept his coke in the bottom drawer of his desk!

Backlash Begins

*T*he raid was quickly forgotten, but Mrs. B would use it as a cautionary tale to all new girls so they didn't dare bring drugs on to the premises. We girls hardly discussed it, as it wasn't a happy memory and we didn't like to scare newcomers unnecessarily. Work continued as normal, men came in and left with a smile, and there was a steady flow till December crept up on us.

Christmas was rapidly approaching, and things were more sociable. Layla and I had been sitting in a pub with a few of her friends that week, and I had been chatting to this guy called David she knew. We were talking about drugs, of all things; he was fascinated that I didn't do any, which was unusual in this town and me being an art student. He thought everyone was taking something. I was in the unique position of knowing what the so-called professionals got up to, as most of them told me while getting dressed after a session! Mostly pot to wind down at the end of the day, or an E for the weekend, nothing too heavy. David was a writer, or so he claimed, and seemed fascinated by the drugs issue. He just didn't get how I didn't need drugs: didn't I want to escape reality and live in a fantasy world sometimes? My reply? I didn't need drugs to escape to a fantasy world, I already lived in one! I didn't mind anyone else taking them, each to their own—if that's what gets you by, who am I to judge? But my life was strange enough as it was, I didn't need anything to help.

"Interesting...I will remember that," was all he said, lost in thought, as he slipped away from our gathering.

I don't think I ever saw him again. I stopped going out as much with Layla after that, always finding excuses. I think it was just dawning on me how bizarre my world was becoming. It was like walking around under a veil, through which I could see out but no one could see in. It's a claustrophobic, uneasy, suffocating feeling, this inner world of paid sex.

I started pulling away from friends and avoiding the possibility of meeting normal people. I was always anxious they might somehow cause me trouble in the future. This was becoming a recurring theme. I found myself starting to skip uni classes, only turning up to the bare minimum. I kept my head down and just got on with my work. Cutting out classmate socializing altogether was easier now that I had moved in with Layla and Sanita. "I'm going out with flatmates" or "It's my turn to cook tonight" were great excuses to fend off any friendly classmates while remaining polite. In reality, there really wasn't any time to socialize in the pub between shifts and study as well but, more importantly, I couldn't always remember who knew what either. In the end, it became much easier simply to stay away altogether.

Christmas was the horniest time of the year, or so it seemed, as the whole of December was totally booked up. Men and women clearly deal with the Christmas rush in very different ways. The only decorations decking the house were us. We would totter out saying hello in diamante necklaces, black panties, long gloves, stockings, just a feather boa to cover our breasts.

They would come in during the day after being pulled around the shops by the wife. Pretending to nip down to the pub for a pint, they would sneak in to see us as their wives finished off the shopping. Many a guy would pop in laden down with bags and needing quick relief, before dashing back out again, feeling much happier.

I was getting to be a popular girl, seeing from eight to twelve clients in a shift. I normally worked a night shift on a Tuesday but would change depending on the rota. I'd always worked on Sundays, as that was the quietest day and no one else wanted to work it. But gradually Sundays had begun to be my busiest day, as I would tell all my regulars that I would definitely be in that day. Layla and Samantha had also started to work that day too, so it became a good day to work, with a more relaxed atmosphere and a fixed group of the best of us, the three top-earning girls at the time.

One Sunday I had been busy all morning, in the knowledge that this was my last shift for a few days and I could get some uninterrupted sleep. The jacuzzi was very relaxing if you'd had a long day and, most importantly, guys loved it too. After being picked I would take the guy downstairs to the spa room and we would both strip off and slide into the water. Chatting was really the only thing we were allowed to do in the jacuzzi, for hygiene reasons, so after a long soak we would head to a room next door and start the massage routine.

It had been a very busy day, and a client wanting the jacuzzi was nothing new. I had already been down there once that morning to share the tub with a client and Suzie. For an extra fiver a regular could spend time in the jacuzzi with two girls of his choice and then decide in the tub which one of us he wanted to go to a room with. The girl who was not needed got the extra fiver. This client had opted for Susie, so I had dried off and tottered back to the girls' lounge to have lunch while she gave the massage.

Later on that day I had my own client happily sitting next to me in the jacuzzi. Stepping out of the tub to reach for a towel, I slipped down the steep wet steps, bumping down each one on my back. I was mortified to have done this in front of my client and I must have been a little dazed, as I didn't know that I had taken the top layer of skin off my backbone; it had started to bleed. My nice client helped me up, but I felt so embarrassed that I shook the incident off, wrapping my bathrobe around me and showing him to our allocated room. I didn't notice the damage I had done till I had finished in the Green Room. I checked it out in the bathroom mirror as my back had started to sting from all the strong chemicals Mr. B put in the jacuzzi to keep it clean. Some girls wouldn't get in, said it made their fanny sore—didn't have the problem myself, mine's bloody water-tight.

I worked the rest of the day but took it easy, staying on top of the guys and lying on my front watching TV in the girls' lounge. When Mr. B came in and saw what had happened to me he wasn't too thrilled at the result, and a gleaming chrome hand-rail appeared down in the spa room overnight. About bloody time!

For me, the run-up to Christmas was the busiest time I had ever had there. I did more shifts than normal to help meet the demand, which was perfect, as it was now the holidays and classes were over. By client eight I was swollen and offered a tight fit. By client ten I was raw and sore and by twelve you get numb! Anyone after that you just can't feel at all—we called it the Xmas feeling...I was lucky if I could sit down the next day. The busiest day, Mrs. B told us, was bound to be the Friday before Christmas—it always was, and nine girls worked that shift to cover. Boy, was Mrs. B right—we even had a bet going on how many guys would come in!

As we got into the last week in December, I fell into a rhythm—home—SLEEP—eat—go back to the bordello—and as things settled into a routine and I continued to pick up regulars, it was only a matter of time before the backlash began. Why was I so popular? The conclusion was that I must be doing extras. The rumour was rife and spread by an overweight girl I will call Big Mouth Emma for the sake of the story. She didn't work much. She had been at the house for a while and was not picking up much custom, which made her stroppy. Unfortunately, it showed as she mumbled hello to waiting customers. It was a shame really, because she was all smiles to everyone else and quite friendly to me, a bubbly girl who would always offer you a cup of tea if she was making one.

She had a pretty face, but that doesn't count for much if you don't smile in those few seconds you have to say hello to guys. I learned early on from Carry that a good smile and a friendly face work wonders, as clients are quite nervous sitting there, waiting for it all to begin. When you are standing in the doorway, a client will take in all of you, normally starting his onceover from the top and travelling down. If you don't smile or if you rush the process, he won't even remember your name, let alone anything else.

Big Mouth Emma—bless her. Having three children hadn't helped her figure. Quite a lot of the girls with children had let their bodies go. They were usually the ones whose bellies would hang over their knickers, but that also applied to some girls who didn't have the baby-wrecked-my-body excuse. Despite all the exercise in the bedroom, the sitting around waiting didn't help; unless you were on active duty most of the time, it was pretty sedentary. The barrel of chocolate biscuits in the kitchen was a killer and the freezer packed with pizzas didn't help either.

Anyhow, being fairly new, the backlash was, I guess, bound to happen. The week before, Layla had warned me: the gripe was mainly due to me taking business away from other girls and she advised me that I should watch my back. The heads-up was helpful; the fact was that everyone had been so friendly I hadn't really thought about it.

Clients can be a fickle lot. You can have a reg for ages, but as soon as a new girl comes along and tickles his fancy, he will swap, that's the game. It doesn't earn you any friends in a house when you are the new girl taking business from a long-timer. I was lucky on the one hand as the bosses were delighted with the custom I was bringing in but unlucky on the other when I had to deal with the waspish fall-out.

I kept my head down all week and was extra friendly, asking if anyone wanted tea when I got up to make some, helping the receptionists check and restock the rooms during quiet spells and folding the towels when they were rushed off their feet. As far as I was concerned, it was always an idea to keep in the good books of the receptionist working on your shift. It all sounds a bit calculated, now I think about it, but everyone knows a moving target is much harder to hit than a sitting duck. You can't really trust anyone in a working house, and jealousy is always the main reason. As long as you don't disobey the rules, keep your head down (excuse the pun), and don't bitch about others, you're normally all right, unless you do something completely stupid or incur the wrath of the other girls.

Mrs. B knew everything that happened in her little domain and, as I had already discovered, she always had one girl being an internal spy in return for favours (new hair cut, extra shifts, etc.).

As soon as Emma had opened her trap and the Bosses found out that she was shit-stirring about me, she was in trouble. Mrs. B knew I wasn't doing anything untoward and, as business came first with her, it didn't take a genius to work out whose side she would be on, given that I was one of her top earners (I earned the house over four times what Big Mouth brought in). If I had been playing up, it would have been a different story—I would probably have been pulled aside, given a firm talking to, and threatened with the sack, as well as being put on the graveyard shifts.

I was the first to arrive for the evening shift. Mrs. B had buzzed me in through the back door, which was unusual, as that was normally a job for the receptionist. I didn't think anything of it as Mrs. B smiled at me, said hi, and, hunched over the phone in her big black woolly cardie, rattled off the names of the girls who would be working that evening to some disembodied voice on the other end.

I padded off to the bathroom, took a shower, and stood in the kitchen, scantily clad, putting the kettle on. Bang! A few of us heard it all kick off in the kitchen and rushed out to the lounge to see what was going on. I had never seen Mrs. B look so angry. With two hands on the back of Big Mouth's head, she had her face jammed up against a mirror on the wall and was shouting at her, the gist being, "Look at yourself! Is it any wonder?" We all froze in our tracks. She's a big woman, Mrs. B, towering over most of the girls, formidable at the best of times, but that day she looked like bloody King Kong on steroids. It was over very quickly and Big Mouth slid down the wall in tears, blubbering as Mrs. B shouted, "Get out, you're fired," and pointed at the door. Emma skulked out, King Kong hot on her heels.

I don't think any of us dared speak—we were all too stunned—so we got straight back to getting ready and drinking tea. I had some notion that Emma had been fired for turning up late again. It was Mrs. B's pet peeve, and even though she had been only two minutes late that evening, it could have been what tipped our employer over the edge.

I didn't find out the real reason till well after Big Mouth had left. No one would tell me what was really going on. It was all hushed whispers and shoulder shrugging. I was a bit shocked when I found out the truth from nineteen-year-old Ricky (that week's new girl, who had worked her first shift with Big Mouth a few days before). Apparently, Big Mouth had been telling the other girls that I did anal and probably unprotected oral and that's why I was so popular—bitch! Ricky, a skinny, gangly thing, had heard everything. She wasn't an obvious threat to Emma and, being the new girl, she was a perfect sponge for soaking up Big Mouth Emma's lies.

So it had nothing to do with the fact I was still fairly new then, still something of a novelty? Or that I was bloody good to my clients? Or smiled properly at every client who came through the door, no matter what they looked like and...OK, the fact that I was still fit and toned really helped...The only other girl with a more toned bod than me was Paris, and she was an aerobic nut who just couldn't sit still. There were lots of reasons I did well, but extras wasn't one of them. Just goes to show that if you shit-stir you should be very careful or it will blow up in your face. Ricky might have been young, but coming in from working the streets, she wasn't as gullible as people supposed. She asked around before she drew any conclusions and I liked that about her.

Big Mouth cornered me in the street a few weeks later after I had wheedled more out of Ricky about what had happened. Looking a bit bedraggled, Big Mouth apologized and asked if I could put in a good word for her. When I told Layla and Sanita about my encounter they were indignant; they couldn't believe she had the nerve to talk to me after all that time slagging me off behind my back.

I still don't understand why she did it. I liked her a lot and thought we got on well. How was my bitch radar so far off?

I have been far more selective in choosing my friends since then. What goes around comes around, and you shouldn't blab and behave badly if you can't take the consequences.

Well, life is one big lesson, and that episode taught me that if a regular client goes with another girl it doesn't mean he doesn't like you or she's stolen him from you, it's just that he fancies a change. It comes with the territory, and another client will come along to take his place. At the end of the day, he's your punter, not your boyfriend, so there is no need to take it personally. Bitching about it and complaining about how much money you have lost solves nothing. Mark, Mr. Security Guard, is another one who was far from loyal. After his over-protective attitude towards me at the club, I bumped into him again. It was perfect timing, as I remember being wound tighter than a spring. I needed to release some sexual tension. Mark, not having to work on the door of the night club till later, had joined the rest of us at our local. We sat and chatted and he wouldn't stop talking about his wife—he sounded like a broken record! I had heard enough. There had been sufficient touching up under the table for me to feel frustrated again, so when he wandered off to the bar I slipped outside without the girls noticing, catching his eye on my way out. Predictably, he followed me to the car park, where I sat on the hood of his car. I started to shiver, but not with anticipation—it was bloody cold on his metal car hood—so he opened the door, saying, as I slid in to the interior, that he knew somewhere nearby that was warmer. He drove us down the road to the telephone exchange, which he had the keys for. He worked there, too, as a security guard, dropping in at night to do checks on the property.

Punching in the code and unlocking the main door, he pushed me ahead of him down the narrow corridor, past walled banks of bleeping, flashing wire panels, and into the empty office at the end. Nothing in there really but two empty desks, a few chairs and a waste-paper bin by the door, but at least it was warm.

Laying me down on one of the desks, he managed to pull my trousers, knickers, and shoes off as I pushed myself up on my elbows to stare at him. He was shaking as he stood there over me, baring his torso as he dropped his jumper to the ground, on to the heap of my discarded clothes. The street light shone strips across his chest through the window blinds. Hearing his zip in the quiet room, I looked at the prominent bulge being released as his jeans hit the floor. I stretched my leg out, toying with the lump in his boxers with my toes. Pushing my foot aside, he pulled down the neck of the strappy top which was covering my waiting breasts and enveloped my nipple with his mouth, sucking the little pink nub till it was protruding, then making his way over to its neighbour to do the same. Not the gentlest, I must say—the clumsy boy was a bit heavy-handed! He left finger bruises all over me, so I had little reminders of what had happened for the whole of the following week! I think he just got carried away. I found out he'd had one hell of a crush on me for months.

I pushed with my foot at the waistline of his boxers and, with his help, they went down. Oh, no...this wasn't going to be easy, I remember thinking! He had a slightly wider girth than Patrick and sought access with frustration, kneeling down, lifting my legs over his shoulders. The whole episode was frustrating enough, but the next day I found out that our second little encounter had become public knowledge. Apparently, Mark had turned up to work at the night club with his shirt inside out, disclosing and embellishing what had happened to the boys. I really wasn't happy, especially as half of what was doing the gossip rounds wasn't even true. I also found out that the other guys had been warned off by him. I was basically no-man's-land without knowing. Retribution was dealt to restore the karmic balance though. Don't you just love it when that happens? There had been someone watching that night in the exchange. A hidden security camera had recorded everyone coming in the entrance. Mark hadn't had a clue about it, as he hadn't had the job long—the next week he was fired for letting an unauthorized person on to the premises.

Becoming a Pro

*C*ebell filled in on one of my weekday shifts, and I was not too happy with the outcome. For some reason she didn't take the money when showing a guy to a room, saying something about him wanting to pay the girls directly instead (I was on a Gemini with Ricky). Sending us in, she forgot to tell me about her little deed. At the end of the session, I asked him if he had paid (like most clients did on weekday shifts) and he assured me he'd paid as normal, so we showed him out after time was up.

It soon became clear he had gone and done a runner with the money! I should have known better, but I felt bad for Ricky, as it had been only her second client, despite it being her second shift and, after all her enthusiasm, she came away empty-handed. Cebell told me not to tell Mr. and Mrs. B about what had happened, and after the Big Mouth incident I didn't want to stir up any more dirt. She wiped the booking from the chart and I put the whole experience down to another lesson learned. Ricky wasn't too upset.

"She ain't playin' with a full deck, is she?" she whispered, and nudged me, pointing in Cebell's direction. It was more a statement than a question. I smiled back at her, feeling a bit weary, and rolled my eyes upward. Despite being new, she had hit the nail on the head. Cebell was a liability.

I found out later that Mr. B would never have been angry with me, as I was one of his favourites. He had a passion for redheads, which I didn't know about until Mrs. B dyed her hair red. No wonder Mrs. B kept an eye on me all the time! I got so used to her glaring out of the corner of her eye that it stopped bothering me after a while. It was either paranoia, or due to the amphetamines she took for her dieting, or so the rumour went. I think it was a bit of both. Mr. B didn't ever try it on and, as I was a good earner with a great record for repeat custom and I didn't cause them any trouble, she let me be.

I got on well with Mr. B, a big hulk of a man, a bit scary-looking, as if he had been in too many fights but had always managed to come out victorious. In his forties, with short brown hair, he was a good man when you got to know him—business was business. As far as I was aware, he hadn't ever had a service from any of the girls. He certainly didn't have wandering eyes or hands—he actually had a lot of respect for us girls. It was clear that he didn't really have any say in the running of the house and seemed just to be there to deal with any problems. Mrs. B was much sterner, she was the boss, and their partnership worked very well.

I got to know Ricky better as the days went by. I liked her, but she was a tad mad. Her Welsh accent rang around the small kitchen. She was a skeletal junkie with badly bleached hair and one-inch black roots, and she was trying to sort her habit, or so she said. Up front and a bit crude, Ricky didn't ever discuss her family but, reading between the lines, it was probable she had been abused as a kid, run away from home as a young girl, and had been fending for herself on the streets ever since. One day I entered the kitchen and caught the tail end of a conversation between her and Sukey. Ricky was talking about a pearl necklace—intriguing! Small gifts and tips weren't unusual. Once I even had a cheeky client who gave me a fiver tip and then asked for £2.50 change so he could feed the parking meter of the wife's car! He'd snuck out while she had been shopping in a department store and popped into the house. No wonder he'd shot his load, showered, and disappeared so quickly. I had yet to receive a gift from a client, but I knew other girls regularly did. To be honest, I knew it was unlikely I'd ever receive a gift, given the kind of men who were in my bunch of regulars. But I'd got the wrong end of the stick. With animated gestures, Ricky was telling Sukey what had just happened in the Green Room.

"He said to me...like...'Would you like me to give you a pearl necklace?' 'Well, yeah,' I said...and then...then he came all over my throat and titties!" She grimaced. "Didn't know what he was meaning...did I, babe?" She threw her hands up in the air. "Wouldn't have said yes otherwise...would I!"

Sukey sat at the sturdy little kitchen table nodding, both hands clasped around a hot chocolate. Ricky carried on ranting while waiting for her microwave meal to ping. Sukey kept shrugging at the questions being thrown her way and looked back at me, raising her eyebrows over the rim of her mug. I don't know what we were supposed to say, but when Ricky was on a roll it was best to let her rant till she ran out of steam. I had discovered that leaving a girl to get a moan off her chest was by far the best course of action—maybe give a hug if there are tears involved but, otherwise, leave well alone. Hell...if I am in a mood or feel grumpy, I just want to lock myself in a room away from everyone till I calm down. I don't like to have verbal squabbles with anyone—what's the point? Especially not in such a highly strung environment. It is a stressful enough job without us bickering among ourselves. Plus, I had a lifetime's experience being a mediator during family squabbles. In fact, I became so skilled at it that my father used to joke that I should be a diplomat! Given the route I have ended up taking, unless the government are looking to employ a *Very* Personal Relations Ambassador, "a bonking emissary" of sorts, I can't see it somehow...

I was getting to know the other girls better, too. Most girls stayed for some time. If they didn't make enough money or the work fucked with their heads too much, they left. New girls would start every now and then and most quit after a few shifts, but the majority of us were long-timers and we grew to know each other well. It's not as though we would sit around discussing clients—we had other things to talk about. Those of us who were students would sit at the kitchen table, where it was quieter, and do homework assignments, or we would lounge about between clients and watch the movie of the day. Our video-player in the lounge was on a loop, so when you missed bits while you were busy you would be able to catch up later. Sometimes we had the music video channel playing in the background. It was very homely and almost felt like dorm life, but just by chatting, listening, and watching the girls in the lounge, you could pick up a lot of useful advice.

It was these girlie moments, making tea, munching biscuits, and chatting, that gave me a much clearer idea of the range of personalities at work in the house. And, boy, did I meet some very different characters. Bella was our motherly, five foot seven dominatrix. She wore the shiniest boots I had ever seen and would swirl cups out with boiling water before making tea to "make sure they were clean." "Your body is your temple and livelihood," I was informed by the ex-nurse in mantra-like fashion. She had a very good point. If you caught something you could not work, as the clinic would inform the house and you would have to take time off till you were clear. Sometimes you had to stop work altogether. A devastating thought...a total waste of sexual opportunities, not to mention the loss of money.

Paris was the house fitness freak, and she was always on the go. Black and in her early twenties, with short hair, she liked fast, expensive cars and was always paying vast sums for car insurance and speeding fines. She had been the one to warn me against wearing perfume when she caught me in the bathroom spraying myself with a girlie floral. Wives might smell it on the guys and that would let the cat out of the bag. They might not come back, and you would lose a client. The tip was to use men's deodorant instead— genius! Paris was canny and always looking for a way to make more money. If she saw an opportunity she would grab it with both hands. I had a feeling that if something wasn't nailed down, Paris would have it, anything so she could spend it on her car. I don't know why, but I really didn't trust her. I don't think many of the girls did. On the whole, we all got on well, but if we met by chance outside the house on the street, we would walk straight past each other, looking the other way, even if we were on our own, passing without saying a word. It was a matter of respect. If one of us had a friend with us it would have been hard to explain how you knew each other, especially if the other girl had called you by your working name. Mrs. B would give us fake names to help protect our identities— mine was Miss S.

It wasn't just the girls I got to know. One of the life-changing things about working in a house, as well as the characters you meet, is that you get a whole new insight into men. I have to admit that, even now, I judge every man I meet on what he likes in bed—not what he does for a living, what he drives, or whether he is rich (although that helps). It is his taste between the sheets that tells me all I need to know. It becomes easy to recognize the little pointers: the overenthusiastic ones, the ones who find certain suggestions you make distasteful but then ask you for something even more off the wall! The confident, cocky ones who are a bit too rough and think they are total shag-meisters when the opposite is true. But the ones with a sense of inner calm, the ones you just know are good in bed, well, they are always the ones who are attached and extremely faithful. I'm rarely wrong. It took a lot of experimenting along the way, but I can sense who will be a good shagging partner for me just by talking to him. It's taken some of the fun out of my personal sex life, but I'm rarely disappointed any more.

Friday 19th December

All-day shift 10:30 a.m.–1 a.m.
3 x Gemini, one with Sally, two with Chloë = £45
14 x normal service = £280
Minus £20 receptionist's fee
Total earned: £305

The pleasant clients were as frequent as the night-mares, and the blond, tanned carpenter in his mid-thirties was every girl's favourite—Mr. Magic Fingers. No hard stabbing or poking action like so many others—why do men do that? It hurts like hell. If you are going to do the poking thing, use your dick, that's what it's for!

The Carpenter would leave the lucky girl with a smile on her face that would last till the end of the shift. Ahhh, those fingers...I remember them well...I would start by giving him the obligatory massage and then he would return the favour, and not a rushed, rough rubdown like some others, who thought they were good at it...No...this was a slow, soft, long rubdown that got me wriggling and horny and that's when his fingers would travel down my body and start the rhythmic rubbing, and just in the right place. Not too hard, not too light, just right, no prompting needed. It didn't take long until I drew him to me, rolling over on my back and finishing what we had started. He was a great start to the shift.

While the Carpenter was everyone's favourite, my particular joy was the Long-Haul Lorry Driver. I sooo used to look forward to him coming in. He would have been driving around Europe for weeks at a time; sounds like a drag, but although the hours were long, the pay was good. When he returned, his first port of call would be the sauna. He was an ash-blond twenty-eight-year-old, eyes hidden behind his rimmed glasses, a grubby baseball hat on his head, and very casually dressed. He was not someone you would notice on the street, well, apart from his towering height. You couldn't see how striking he was until he removed his glasses and cap. That's why most of the girls thought he was nondescript, but those who knew him would enthuse about how gorgeous he was. After a while of trying us all out, he started to request me, and I became his official favourite. I didn't mind the ribbing I got from the other girls, he was my tall secret. Under all his casual street camouflage, I swear that guy could have given any male model a run for his money and he would have won hands down. (And beautiful hands he had, too.)

Good looks on their own don't normally affect me but, with him, it was the total package—he knew just how to please and that was the clincher. He was too good a client to lose. I made sure I booked specific shifts on days when I knew he would be back in the country, and if I had to skip

an important class at uni, then so be it. Despite my enthusiasm, I didn't ever think about meeting him outside the
house for a date. Work was work and that was it and,
besides, it was still a small town.

He always followed the same routine. He'd start off with
a long shower, and I would be there to hold a towel for him
as he got out. It was always a long booking, normally two
hours, and once he had settled in The Parlour, I would
bring him a coffee. He would lie on his front as I gave him
a long, slow massage, turning him over and sucking him
off to start with, releasing all the built-up pressure. Lying
together on the bed, we chatted and joked with each other
as he stroked my body. Inevitably, he would soon be hard
and I would pounce on him, riding him slowly till he had
had enough. After that we would tumble on the bed and
talk until our time was up. I would show him out the back
way and he would kiss me on the forehead as he left.

I could relax with him, taking my time, knowing he
wasn't going to shag me senseless, as if he was going for a
world record, and I could guarantee that I would not be
sore for the rest of my shift. A long, slow screw...lovely, just
what I needed to cheer up a boring day. But it did make for
a tiring week when he was on form.

By this time, I was getting on really well with the girls
and it got to the point where I would look forward to going

into work, to catch up on gossip and meet any new girls. I felt more at home there in the girls' lounge than at our flat down the road—it was like an extended coffee morning, with occasional moments of activity. You could always find someone for a chat, there was always something happening, and if you needed any kind of advice or help it was freely given. Of course, there was the odd girl you avoided going to with anything too personal, as you knew it would be around the room as soon as you left but, on the whole, I trusted the girls more than my student friends. In some cases, for example with Layla, I trusted the girls like family. I'm very loyal to my close friends and know they will be the same back.

So I knew for certain the girls would be behind me that day when The Smelly Farmer, who I had seen twice before, walked in and accused me of giving him crabs during our session the previous week! He made his accusation to our resident aerobic drama queen Paris, after he picked her out of our "hello" line to give him a massage.

She really didn't want to see him; no one ever did. His fingernails were always filthy, and it didn't seem to matter if he had a shower or not, because he would always come out stinking just as badly as he had before. After turning him over after a quick rubdown, Paris promptly ran screaming from the room.

She burst into the girls' lounge. *"Crabs...oh my god, crabs,"* she screamed, brushing herself down and jumping around in a deranged fashion. *"He said you gave him crabs."* She pointed at me as she headed straight for the shower in the girls' bathroom.

I couldn't believe the accusation and turned, to find everyone in the room staring at me. All the girls knew I had just been to the clinic for a check-up the day before and had been given the all-clear. Carry and Suzie had even teased me a couple of hours earlier, saying that I seemed to live in the clinic. I probably did visit the clinic more than any girl in the house, at least once every three months, if not more. I would rather know than not. I lived in fear of there being the slightest chance I had something and could pass it on to someone else.

Louise, the receptionist on that shift, had the pleasure of telling The Smelly Farmer there was no way I could have given him crabs. She asked him to leave and come back only when he was clean. "Until then you will have to shag your sheep!" she called after him as he left. We could all hear this from the corridor and fell about laughing. For the rest of the night, the chat was of shaving to keep crabs at bay. Suzie happily showed off her newly waxed line of muff fluff to all and sundry. I hadn't thought of shaving down below till that day, but most of the other girls were clean-shaven or waxed. Guys didn't seem bothered either way. But I followed suit, leaving a small triangle, just to prove, when asked, that my collar matched my cuffs.

That Friday before Christmas, groups of men were piling in; it was their last day at work. Money was burning a hole in their pockets from payday, and they were merry from Christmas lunches at work. I didn't get to say hello much or sit down at all, it was absolutely draining: when I came back up with the towels and rubbish, I was sent straight back down to another room.

Louise and Polly were both on reception that day and were nearly as rushed off their feet as we were. I even had guys waiting over an hour just to see me!! The total number of men to cross the threshold that day was 127, and I saw a total of seventeen in one shift! I lost count after the first twelve, the whole day was a bit of a blur, but the tips were great, which was about the only thing that made it worth doing.

Sunday 21st December

All-day shift 10:30 a.m.–1 a.m.
13 x normal service + tips (including a regular, Brian, and the
Analytical Chemist) = £295
Minus £20 receptionist's fee
Total earned: £275

*I*t was the end of December when I stumbled upon The Analytical Chemist. He was a young, cute redhead, an utter boffin but great fun and, most importantly, a damn good shag too (confirmed by Layla, as he would pick her when I wasn't around). Every redheaded male I have ever been with has been good in bed. They are so gentle and eager to please, they just seem to know what to do and do it till you beg them to stop (in a good way). He liked the Mirror Room because he enjoyed watching himself in action from all sides, and he especially loved the view from the mirror overhead. He sat in the bath and waited till I came in, splashing me as I opened the door. I gave him a hard rubbing down when he did that. Tumbling on the bed and taking off my bra, he picked up the oil bottle from the bed, rubbing first my back and then moving around my thong. He loved to fill the furrow between my buttocks with oil and slither up and down my back. Normally this would piss me off, as all that oil is a terrible mess to clean up, but he was careful not to get it on the bed and, anyway, it was covered with a towel and a paper bedroll sheet for extra protection. My thong, on the other hand, would need a very good washing afterwards. He turned me over and straddled me, imprisoning my legs between his thighs. He sucked and played with my nipples as I stretched, watching in the mirror above. I was eager to play with his hard cock and wiggled from underneath him to get a firm hold, sucking lustfully away till I changed position. It didn't last long with me on top; he wanted to ride me. On all fours is how we ended it, him grasping me from behind and thrusting away till he was sweaty and spent. What a great way to end the year.

I only saw him about five times in all, and it was the same routine every time. He had to leave the area to go and work abroad for two years. He said he would send me postcards from Germany, but I didn't believe he would remember to, until two months later, when Mrs. B handed me a postcard addressed to the house with my name on it, saying simply, "Wish you were here!" I stuck it on the wall in the girls' bathroom and it made me smile every time I walked by, no matter what kind of shitty day I was having.

Happy Days

*R*ight...I am counting down the days to Venice, I have enough money for four months' rent and loads of presents for my family...Phew...what a relief my shifts were over till the new year. Now I could relax and was really looking forward to the celebrations—not so much the bickering and family fighting that went with it, but the break from the sauna. The year had ended with its fair share of drama. Life in the house was a strange thing—one girl has a damn good day and another has the day from hell. One day, Jane arrived at the lounge door, holding her rubbish bag from a job, looking as pale as a sheet and shaking.

Oh dear—the job was definitely fucking with her head that day. We all looked up as she blubbered, "Condom broke! It broke! Oh, fuck, not on the pill! Wrong time! Ohhh, fuck!!"

"Shit," was the chorus. Layla went over to hug her, and they went into the bathroom to talk.

You could hear the sobbing in the lounge, and I bet "Thank fuck it wasn't me" was going through everyone's heads—it certainly was mine. Poor cow. Now, a girl will go two ways if that happens: a) hysterical or b) quiet. Jane was about to get as hysterical as any girl I have known, and she lost the plot so much so that the recep, dithery Cebell, rang Mrs. B to come and deal with the situation. Jane was still in hysterics when Mrs. B arrived, and she ushered Jane upstairs to her flat to try and calm her down. It must have worked, as the sobbing subsided. After that, the lounge was rather quiet, so a music video was put on to dispel the low mood. Jane came down some hours later after a shower and a nap and quietly collected her stuff with Mrs. B, who helped her into a cab. It was the last straw for both of them—Jane had dramatically quit, again—but this time it really was the last we heard from her.

No two ways about it, the job was a psychological head-fuck. If you can't put the profession in a box, it can drive you crazy—you have to switch off. At work you need to be in role all the time, a sort of invincible version of the real you. The client must never sense weakness, and it's all about body language; they need to know they can't walk all over you (unless that's what they are paying for!). That's the main reason girls have working names: it helps you to become someone else and protects your real mental state and sense of self. You can be as bold, brash, and feisty as your persona allows you to be, even if it's nothing like the real you. Unfortunately for Jane, she was always totally Jane and just couldn't separate her real life from her working one. Her separation problem wasn't helped by the fact that she didn't like either life in the first place. And there's just not much you can do about that...

I went home to spend Christmas with my family after I had caught up on my sleep, done a last dash to the shops, and wrapped huge stacks of pressies with big bows. I hadn't seen my family for a few weeks now; I had told them that I had a few Christmas jobs in different shops which had kept me away till the day before Christmas Eve. This had to be the story, as uni had ended well before, a few weeks back...but they were none the wiser and, now I was back, I tried to forget about the Big Bordello. It felt a bit weird to be home, as I was used to doing what I wanted, staying up really late, eating what I chose, going out without telling people where I was going. It was annoying my mum hugely, as she was used to bossing me around. She was also a bit unnerved by my annoying habit of jumping out of my seat every time the door bell rang—it had the same ring as the one that called the girls to say a kinky hello at work. I also had to readjust to answering her when she called out my real name!

A week or so later I escaped Christmas, a huge family war not having broken out, and brought my sack full of "practical" Christmas presents back to the flat to start a new year. Well, I suppose six bottles of washing-up liquid was useful, if a slightly strange choice of Christmas gift.

Both Layla and Sanita were there when I arrived back and greeted me with a big hug. As we all had a few days to go till our lessons started and hadn't planned any shifts, we were at a loose end. I really should have phoned the house and taken a shift to boost my Venice and car fund, but I wasn't in the mood to launch straight back in. We went out with student friends, dressed up as tarts (which wasn't difficult) for a New Year party. Layla and Sanita even propositioned the taxi driver on the way there as an alternative to paying the fare. He took it in good humour, which was ironic, because I have a feeling Sanita actually meant it and forgot she was supposed to be in fancy dress. We all came back alone. I really couldn't be bothered, as the only guy I met who I really liked the look of turned out to be a drunken prick who loved himself. Shame, if he'd kept his mouth shut he might have got lucky.

Only one thing for it: a shopping trip to the sex shop. I have no idea why, but I was in desperate need of a good vibrator for the days I was not working. I also wanted to pick up some porn—girls are curious too, you know! I just found that I was so damn horny all the time, like a cat on heat.

Layla and I headed off to a dirty little shop we had heard about from passing clients, our curiosity aroused by the good things they had said. We were both slightly apprehensive as we entered—Sanita refused to come with us on the grounds that she was just plain scared!

Entering the dimly lit shop, we were faced with an array of coloured rubber and butt plugs, magazines, and strange objects I didn't have the courage to ask about, let alone work out what I needed to do with them. We tiptoed around the shop, picking up a few vibrators and jumping when Layla set one off by accident. We tried nipple clamps on the skin between our thumb and fingers, both deciding we were against them. How can something that bloody well hurt so much be remotely sexy (something I asked myself more and more). We glanced at the magazines but were distracted by a shifty-looking man sidling through the front door. He took one look at us and ran straight back out! He looked more nervous than we felt, which made us giggle, much to the annoyance of the little weird bald guy trying to read his paper and leaning on a tiled glass cabinet. I flicked through a mag I had plucked randomly from the shelf. One look told me it was from the gay section—it was the man-on-man action that gave it away; they were fit but not really my type. Layla was back at the vibrators again and picked out a contender—a medium-sized blue-rubber affair. I had my eye on a black, ribbed, solid plastic one with a gold tip. It looked a bit scary but had a very strong vibration, which was sure to make me numb if I wasn't careful. Could be interesting...

Sunday 11th January 1998: New Year, Back to the House

All-day shift 10:30 a.m.–1 a.m.

15 x normal service + tips (including the Posse of Four + £20 tips altogether; Will—£5 tip; Peter—£10 tip) = £335

Minus £20 receptionist's fee

Total earned: £315

J started the year with my four-strong fan club—a farmer, a volunteer worker, a horse trainer, and a banker. They were friends and would usually come in together before going out for dinner and then to a casino. Occasionally, they would come to the house separately, begging me not to tell the others about their visit. I don't know if they had a pact only to come to the sauna together, but if they did they all broke it.

I was the only girl they came to see. Supposedly, it had something to do with my enthusiasm...obviously, I had worked out early on that the more enthusiastic I acted, the quicker they came and went—if you know what I mean. On a slow night this would piss the girls off, as my posse would plonk themselves down on the few sofas in the foyer to wait and see me and no one else.

They were a handful, the lot of them. There was always one who delighted in trying to finger the hole he shouldn't—just what I needed: more hassle with travelling hands. It was well worth it, though, as it produced an instant £80 and, with the tips (a fiver each), it rounded up to an easy, guaranteed £100. With no bruises on me the next day either, that's what I called easy money.

Back to Uni

*T*he next day, a bright Monday afternoon, I stumbled into class. I had just missed an important talk from some local oil-painter. I wasn't too fussed as our classes were pretty open—you could breeze in and out as you pleased, and no one had really noticed I wasn't there. I was knackered anyway. My posse of four were an exhausting lot.

Natasha popped up out of nowhere, with Sebastian, the best-looking guy on our course, at her side. I hadn't seen much of her since that day I'd helped with her desk.

"You OK? Look a bit peaky," she said, feeling my forehead.

"Fine, just bloody tired—could do with some food, though." My stomach grumbled to prove the point. Dashing out to try and catch the talk, I had skipped lunch.

"Sebastian and I were going to get a snack, you coming? We can fill you in on the talk." I nodded to Sebastian and trailed after them, Natasha gabbling on about light and form or some such thing.

"Look a bit pale, lass," Sebastian whispered in my ear. "Don't think all that black baggy clothing suits you at all, makes you look too pale and a bit ill."

Squeezing his arm, I said, "I'm fine—just a late night is all."

"Date?"

"No, Sebastian..."

"I got this friend that loves redheads."

"Good for him, not interested," I answered back. Like I had time for extracurricular activities; and after the night I'd just had, men were the last thing on my mind—let alone giving it away for free to some geeky student mate of his.

"OK," he smiled.

We shuffled along the buffet queue, picked out a few things for our trays, paid, and plonked ourselves down on the sofas at one end, Natasha next to me and Sebastian opposite.

"So, how is it not having to live in halls and escaping the family Christmas chaos?" Sebastian asked, picking up his burger and taking a bite. He was a handsome, blond, happy-go-lucky chap, but a pain in the ass when he asked questions like that. I was truly paranoid as it was; he could have asked anything and I would have been suspicious.

"Fine, gives me space to create. How's Harry?" Counter a question with a question, always a good way to deflect—thanks, Carry!

"Still heard nothing, think he's back with the parents, doing Open University."

Sebastian's pager started vibrating. "Girlfriend calling?" asked Natasha. "Yep," he said as he dashed off, burger in hand. "Later."

"Can't believe he's still infatuated with her. Girls are swooning all over him, and he continues to chase a girl 100 miles away," squeaked Natasha.

"She probably does anal." Oh god, it just slipped out. Natasha spat her Coke over her salad. Oh, crap, I can't believe I said that. Must be very tired, and momentarily forgot who I was talking to. It was a standard joke with Layla and Sanita that if a guy was hung up on a girl we couldn't stand she was probably a back-door bitch.

Natasha was giggling and trying to mop up her Coke. She laid her hand on my knee. I looked down at it. Oh ohhh…here we go. Maybe Ethan had been right when he'd told me she was a fan of mine.

"So you don't really fancy Sebastian then?" she purred.

Double crap, I could see where this was going. All girls and women fancied the pants off our class stud, so she put two and two together and got her sums wrong, thinking that because I wasn't interested in him, I must fancy women. I could see it ticking over in her brain. I think she was trying to pick me up as some kind of same-sex experiment.

Oh dear. I had sort of seen this coming. One minute we're friendly, next I'm sure she's hitting on me, especially given the hand still in my lap. Had to sit with her on the sofa and gently turn her down with a big speech on how much I fancied men. After that I gave her a wide berth.

Sebastian's mate might not be a bad idea for cover, I thought, but then could I really be bothered? I had enough sex as it was at the moment, I really didn't need complicated relationship sex on top of everything else.

Tuesday 13th January

All-day shift 10:30 a.m.–1 a.m.
15 x normal service (including John; Chinese Peter; another
Chinese regular—£5 tip; The Pacemaker—a grey-haired regular;
2 x Garys—and 2 x £10 tips; the Indian—£10 tip) = £335
Minus £20 receptionist's fee
Total earned: £315

The Pacemaker was old, with grey hair and wrinkly skin, but his smart suit, tie, and shoes, all displayed neatly on the Green Room sofa, gave the impression of someone younger. I started the massage while the music played softly. The volume knob by the bed had been turned down low by a previous occupant so, other than the soft music, all I could hear was a loud ticking from his watch—or so I presumed. I turned him over and quite matter-of-factly said, "My...you've got a loud watch," looking down at his wrist. He took off the watch, placing it on the side table and commented, "Oh, it might not be that," and pointed to his heart. In the dim light all I could see was a small silver scar, but that made me nervous, and what made it worse was that, when I continued to suck his cock, the ticking got faster. Glad I knew CPR. Now, was that two compressions to one breath...or two breaths to one compression? All this was going through my head as my mouth was full and, to make it worse, when I climbed on top, the ticking seemed to escalate out of control. He came and, to my great relief, the tick tick started to slow down. I didn't want to be known as the girl who shagged a guy to death—don't know, though: it might have been good for publicity.

"I was really worried back there, darling," I said, in what was the understatement of the year. I was actually more than a little concerned, I had nearly wet myself!

"Yes," he gasped, "so was I—first time I have done that since I had it fitted...would have been a grand way to go out, though, wouldn't it?"

He showered, I helped him on with his shoes, tied his laces, and showed him out, very much alive and full of life as he bounded off.

Note to self: brush up on my first-aid skills!

Day Off

A few days later, I was chilling out at the flat, sitting on the sofa watching some morning TV, when Sanita walked in carrying a big box of tissues. "Hello, stranger!" I greeted her as she blew her nose. "Cold?" I asked, thinking she looked under the weather. She nodded.

"Mmm, wrong time of the month too," she muttered. Sanita could never manage to work when she had her period.

"Ah, that makes sense—I thought it was strange you weren't down at the house, I've certainly never known a simple cold to stop you." Sanita blew her nose again, looking sorry for herself. "Have you called in?" I asked, and again she nodded.

Usually, I never saw Sanita at the weekend. She worked mostly on Saturdays and got in very late on a Saturday night, practically Sunday morning, and I would leave early that morning, not returning till late myself, if not early Monday.

I budged up on the sofa to make room for her so we could both watch the soap opera on TV. The characters on the box were discussing a wedding, and Sanita was smiling.

"You *must* be hormonal—you're smiling at a cheesy wedding."

"I want one." I handed her another tissue.

"Didn't your folks try to marry you off, and didn't you say no?" I questioned, one eyebrow raised.

"He was a prick, old and ugly...eeew. But if married, I wouldn't have to work and my family would get off my case. I've heard it's an easy life looking after kids." I stared at her as she blew her nose again.

"You're weird. I'm just making tea—fancy a hot-water bottle when I boil the kettle?"

"Yeah, please, that would be great," she sneezed.

Who would have thought Sanita wanted to get married and sprogged up? Certainly not me. Layla had stirred and was on the hunt for her morning coffee fix when I stepped into the kitchen. She looked pretty rough too.

"Sanita really wants to get married. Did you know that?" I asked her.

Layla simply shrugged. "She's a weird woman."

"That's what I said." I refilled the kettle and reached under the sink for a hot-water bottle. Layla heard Sanita sneeze in the living room and put two and two together.

"Bloody hell, what's with us—she's not on too, is she?!" Layla slurped her coffee.

"Mmm, and she has a cold. We'd better stock up on the paracetamol if we're all feeling low this week—we'll all catch it." I pulled cups off the draining board.

"Lovely! Won't Mrs. B be happy!" Layla laughed.

"Echinacea as well?" I asked as I waited for the kettle to boil.

"Yeah, Kiwi fruit too, can't harm," said Layla, shuffling off.

Tuesday 20th January

All-day shift 10:30 a.m.–1 a.m.
10 x normal service + tips (including 5 regulars, Naz—£3 tip;
Short Spiky Hair—£5 tip; Chinese Mabel and difficult Indian
who marked me) = £208
Minus £20 receptionist's fee
Total earned: £188

*T*he Cheeky Chinese guy had no names, so I gave him one...Mabel. He had a very dry sense of humour (if you can call it that). Every time he chose me it was a surprise, particularly as he would hardly say a word. Most guys will at least have a natter back when you say something; for example, when you ask how their day has been most will say, "Fine, thanks, all the better for seeing you," or the cliché, "It's been one hell of a day, I'm so stressed out I need a little bit of relief." Not Mabel. He was one of those people who gave you one-word answers back, if you were lucky—most of the time he would just grunt. It wasn't as if his English was bad—I had heard him talk to the receptionist perfectly well.

I couldn't get what he did or even his name out of him. I didn't understand why he was so secretive or couldn't just give a false name like everyone else (most will stick to something simple like John: always wondered if that's why some girls call punters johns), given that I have normally forgotten what a guy has said by the time they're in the shower and I am tidying up.

On the second occasion he picked me, he was on the staircase following me to one of the rooms when I told him that I had to call him something. He said that he didn't care what I called him. "OK," I said, "you be careful or, as you're pursing your lips like an old granny in a bad mood, I'll end up calling you Mabel or something." He said he truly didn't care and I ushered "Mabel" into the Parlour. It was funny, as he looked nothing at all like a woman. I never could work out why he always came back for my sarcastic abuse; he must get off on it was all I could think. He wasn't one of my favourite clients and certainly not one of my best tippers. In fact, he was a little demanding—pushing me around where he wanted me and most often leaving at least a finger bruise or two. But, saying that, he wasn't one of my worst or most hated guys either. The rough bastards could be much worse than him.

The Regs

I had some time off that week to catch up with some class work. I had an important exam coming up and a term project to work on before my next shift. I also needed to catch up on my sleep. By February I was struggling with classes, as I just wasn't getting enough rest. The days when I fell asleep at my desk in a noisy classroom proved that it was getting hard to juggle work and uni. The night shift during the week and a full day at the weekend were taking their toll. You might only work one day, but it's a bloody long and physical day; you need one day afterwards to sleep and then another fully to recover. But the fact was the money was great, and I had Venice all saved for by then. Plus, I was actually enjoying myself!

I was living very well on £100 a week, meaning I could pocket the rest. It went straight into my car fund. The car cost about 200 fucks in the end; we measured everything that way. Two clients paid the rent each week, the same for food. As I didn't spend anything on cigarettes or booze and not much on course supplies for class (I had stocked up in bulk as it was cheaper), I had a car in no time.

It was great, as I didn't have to take the train home to visit my family any more, and I felt safer driving from A to B rather than walking or taking taxis. Actually, waiting for taxis to turn up was the worst. I spent most of the time wondering if I had "done" the driver at the bordello some time in the past and if he was going to be a problem or not.

Getting and keeping regulars was one of the best ways of staying on top, even if that meant being nice to those you couldn't stand. I had picked up quite a few regulars but, unfortunately, not all of them were pleasant. My least favourite ones, and I had quite a lot, liked me because I looked like a little girl, and they would bounce me on their knee and get me to call them daddy or teacher. Not many of the girls could deal with that, as most of them had children. Can't really blame them...I wasn't too happy with it myself.

I tried to see the positive side—at least if they were seeing me they were leaving the neighbour's children alone, right? I knew that at least one little girl was safe, as a certain guy came to see me every week and talked about his neighbour's nine-year-old. He would go on about stealing her white underwear from the line, and how he watched her and didn't need to touch her because he had me, and I looked like her. I eventually managed to find out where he lived, so if he stopped coming in, I could at least try to inform the police that there might be a problem. I have no idea if they would have taken me seriously—what I do can colour people's perceptions.

You can't really blame people when you see and read all the crap about lying, thieving, junkie whores in the media—if I was a cop I probably would take anything I said with a huge pinch of salt too. You never hear about the majority, the girls who have a heart of gold and are working to support their children.

In the end, to my huge relief, my regular's neighbours moved. He was devastated, said no one could take her place, and he didn't need to see me any more. He never came in again, but I saw many like him. You learn to turn off and be someone else; it helps, it's the only way I could cope with it.

Then there were the dirty, smelly clients, the ones who didn't think it was necessary to shower but would want you to do so in front of them to make sure you were clean! Don't think I could have been any cleaner if I tried. I'm surprised I didn't squeak as I walked down the corridors as it was. The only ones who didn't offend me when they asked me to wash were the Japanese. Cleanliness is their thing; they are spotless. I do love the Japanese—great clients.

The one unhygienic regular I really hated dealing with was known as Donkey Dick, not (as he thought) because he was that well endowed, more because he smelled like donkey's bits. Eeeww...A filthy, extremely fat, dirty, smelly guy who would bend you over anything in the room, putting you in every position he could think of. His favourite position with me (they changed depending on the girl) was me on all fours on the wheeled foot stool, and he would push me around the room, as if we were in a bizarre wheelbarrow race, him in me from behind.

Pouncing on me the moment I was in the room, he didn't ever want a massage and would try sticking his ugly, lumpy stiffness in me as soon as he could. Whether I had managed to take my undies off or not, he would just pull aside the offending fabric and proceed to pound away! He would pull out completely and push it in again while stretching me for better access—or he would just sit on me, shoving himself in my face to suck, till my jaw ached. Oh, yeah...and he liked to stick the end of a biro down the eye of his smelly knob, too; he liked the pain, apparently.

The hilarious thing was that he really reckoned he was some kind of sex god! Somehow he found out what we called him and took it as some sort of compliment! That made us laugh even more! What kind of sex god doesn't wash and thinks that's sexy? His excuse was that if he smelled OK, his wife would know he was up to no good! He talked about his wife non-stop, bragging that she was a gorgeous blonde bombshell, lucky to have him. He even brought her picture in for us to see.

Tuesday 17th February

All-day shift 10:30 a.m.–1 a.m. (extra shift instead of Sukey)
10 x normal service + tips = £230
Minus £20 receptionist's fee
Total earned = £210

I had a call that night from Mrs. B and the news wasn't good—she asked if I could cover Sukey's shift for the next day, as she was in hospital. As far as I knew, Sukey wasn't ill—if someone was, you normally knew about it. I was particularly worried as, that morning, over breakfast, Sanita had said she'd seen Sukey with a black eye on her Saturday shift and Mrs. B had sent her home. Now she was in hospital, and it didn't take a genius to work out why.

Nobody mentioned anything when I arrived at the house in the morning, which was a bit odd—no news is never good news, and it's always worrying when even the gossips are quiet. And the day was only to get odder.

He was quite an ordinary guy, very pleasant, oldish, grey hair, and no trouble. He hadn't stood out as particularly different until he brought out a camera and a dildo. He didn't want face shots, just down below with the vibrator in use. I hadn't noticed either the camera or the dildo till the deed was done and then he asked me if I did extras. I was baffled—hadn't he just come? I investigated—yep, he definitely had. What he was actually asking was whether I would take an extra tenner tip for one shot of me using the dildo. Ahhh, that kind of extra...! Hell, it was only one shot, so why not...couldn't see the harm. I did the deed and showed him out with time to spare and a £10 note tucked in my bra. Only saw him the once—I like to think the photo kept him occupied.

The day ended with some depressing news. Sukey had been severely beaten by her husband and was black, blue, and broken in hospital. Mrs. B had been to the hospital to bring Sukey some flowers, and when she got back she told one of the receptionists what had happened. Mrs. B felt guilty about sending her home after a shift when she was going back to an abusive household, and wasn't saying much more on the matter, so no one really knew what was going on. Most girls were shocked and worried for Sukey— she was a popular girl in the house and had two cute kids. Yes: no news was definitely not good news.

Sunday 22nd February

All-day shift 10:30 a.m.–1 a.m.
2 x Gemini with Samantha = £30
12 x normal service + tips (including one regular, Brian, and a nearly normal half hour with The Councillor) = £245
1 hour with Chinese Lee = £40
Minus £20 receptionist's fee
Total earned: £295

The most annoying client ever had to be The Councillor with Good Intentions. I knew he was trouble the moment I walked into the Yellow Room and he was still dressed! It had been a bad day already, so he hadn't caught me in the best of moods. I'd already been messed around that morning by two guys in very quick succession. One had poked me painfully (wandering hands yet again) and the other, very well endowed, had basically jumped on me the moment I entered the room and had gone at it for the whole half an hour! All I wanted now was an easygoing client.

But that's not what I got. He sat me down on the bed with him when I walked in and launched into his long and pompous speech. If I was being held against my will, he would get me out of here. He thought I was too young! (I was twenty-one at this point...old fart probably needed glasses!) He rambled on. I couldn't possibly want to do this job of my own free will, someone must be pressuring me, or I must be desperate! He carried on, saying they had been talking in his council offices and he had come to see how he could rescue us! God, spare me from well-meaning old farts! Get this: "You don't have to do anything you don't want to do." Nodding calmly, I said, "I know," and, tugging at his belt, I continued with, "Take your pants off and stop teasing me or I will have to give you your money back." I told him he was wasting my time, and if he didn't find me attractive enough, he shouldn't have picked me. I told him it was upsetting if he didn't put out and I was starting to find him really offensive.

How dare he judge us like that, thinking we were scared, imprisoned, powerless women who needed rescuing! Some of the girls I had worked with had had abusive partners and were managing somehow to gather the money and the strength to leave them. They were the girls who had gone to his beloved council and to the social services for help, and it was the council and social services who turned out to be the very people who had turned a blind eye to their plight and threatened to take their children away. The house was an environment they felt they could control, one in which they felt protected and earned enough to keep their children safe at home. They found the courage to come to the house and work and that took guts. How dare this man unload all his misguided, ill-informed views on me...sanctimonious toad!

I got my own back the only way I knew. I jumped on him, told him I was horny, and that he had to at least let me give him a blow-job. Trying to undress him, I told him my time was nearly up and he would lose me my job, taking so long. I would be out on the street at the end of the day and it would all be his fault. Divine retribution: he ejaculated in the rubber the moment I sucked him...he couldn't even last. I tidied up and showed him out. He hadn't been expecting that...got waaaay more than he bargained for when he picked me to try and rescue!

Earlier that day, one of the girls had informed us that she had just seen the manager of the local McDonald's, where she had picked up some lunch, and he told her she didn't have to do this kind of thing any more, that he could get her a job at his place shovelling chips and making up Happy Meals. Hilarious! She thanked him profusely but said that she was perfectly happy where she was. Hanna was normally quiet, but she was nearly wetting herself laughing, retelling the story. We all found it hysterical, as Hanna was a qualified architect for a big firm in the next town—how ironic, given her education and career, that Mr. Big Mac looked down his nose and took pity on her and the rest of us! There are quite a few souls out there, women and men alike, who think we need "saving." Sometimes it's quite funny, but after a while it gets bloody annoying.

Wednesday 25th February

Evening shift 6 p.m.–1 a.m. (called in as sick cover)
7 x normal service + tips (including Phone Sex Guy; 2 x
Chinese—one £20 tip, one £5 tip) = £165
No receptionist fee
Total earned = £165

This shift was another contender for the "only saw him once but it was memorable" category: Phone Sex Guy. As per usual we had all said our kinky hello in the reception room. As he had requested me, I picked him up from the reception room, gathered the necessary things from the bathroom, and took him upstairs. He was on his mobile at that point, so I beckoned to him as I didn't want to interrupt, especially as I could hear a female voice on the other end. I took him to our allocated room, the Velvet Room, at the top of the stairs. Don't know why I had to take him up—it was normally the recep's job, but she must have been busy that night. He was still on the phone when we entered the room, and I closed the door behind me. He looked around and started animatedly describing to the girl on the other end of the line what the room was like. Her name was Cathy. At this point I was not sure if he was on a kinky chatline or if he was bragging to a girlfriend or something. He asked me with raised eyebrows what happened next—typical, a weird newbie...I told him to take his things off, leave them on the sofa—yes, and his pants too—and to lie face down on the bed, where I would start with a massage. I sauntered over to him and draped my short gown on the end of the bed, and all the while he was describing everything that was happening to this Cathy. Still with the phone clamped to his ear, we got half-way through the massage when he started moaning. He handed the phone over to me, thrusting it into my hand. "Hi." Well, what else could I say?

"Ride him hard for me," Cathy instructed. I handed the phone back and rolled him over to start what had been requested. I was starting to wonder if the phone was going to be permanently attached to his head throughout our time together, but when I climbed on top he put the phone down as he couldn't concentrate on two things at once. Some minutes later, with some more groaning, it was over...whatever floats your boat. That one comes high on my list of the strangest things I have done.

Friday 27th February

All-day shift 10:30 a.m.–1 a.m.
Gemini with Layla = £15
17 x normal service + tips (including Guy from Hong Kong—
£10 tip; 4 regulars: a Grey-hair; the Milk Man; a Chinese Peter
with Buck Teeth—£10 tip; Taxi-Driver Mike—£10 tip) = £370
Minus £20 receptionist's fee
Total earned: £365 (the best day's earnings so far!)

The Taxi Driver was a reg. He would usually come in after one in the morning, just as we were shutting up shop; this was when his cab shift ended, and he would pop in after a particularly stressed day. He must have been in his late forties, tall, fit, with thinning blond hair and a shiny gold front tooth, deep-tanned from head to foot, with a thick white tan line around his middle. Not sure where he went abroad, but wherever it was, it must have been damn hot. I would work out the knots in his back and neck for most of the session. My hands would ache from treading away at his soft, wrinkly skin, covered here and there with the odd faded tattoo. We talked very little as he relaxed, he liked it that I didn't babble on as he had heard it all day in the cab. He would lie there till he was well and truly aroused and could no longer lie on his front. I would jump on his stiff member when he rolled over. It was over and done with really fast, a quick suck before he got impatient and rolled on top to ride me. Not drunk, no fuss, no hassle: the perfect way to finish the shift.

Unfortunately, I once ran into him outside the sauna. I was in a small shop when he walked in, with a young boy who must have been his son. He stood there stock-still, stunned, as I walked around him and out of the shop without so much as a backward glance. He didn't come in after that; I can only think I scared him off with that brief encounter.

Social Intercourse

*B*y the time March came around I was really looking forward to the trip to Venice, especially as my test results had just come back clear from the Chinese prick incident. I didn't have to push it to the back of my mind any more and my little saving fund was now back to being my car fund rather than the rainy-day fund it had become. I felt like a weight had been lifted from my shoulders—phew!

I wasn't going to dwell on it. Actually, most girls don't like to talk about the negative side to the job, particularly in front of the new ones. My attitude has always been that the best way to give the newcomers any info is to send them to the docs—that way they get the cold, hard facts drummed into them from the very beginning. It's bad enough dealing with the difficult clients, the rough hands, and the attitude, without dwelling on the ifs and buts.

Anyway, the trip to Venice was fast approaching and I had already repacked my suitcase several times. My very flashy camera, with a long zoom, was packed safely in its own bag with enough batteries and film to cover every street in the city. Counting down the days was tedious. I had booked the week off work for the trip, scheduling to start again four days after I got back. I couldn't wait to go.

The thought of it was definitely keeping me going through my shifts at work—in fact, I couldn't really focus on much else, especially not on Ricky, who on one particular day was rambling on as I got ready in the bathroom for my next shift.

"I've bin doing so well." She looked up from the cold tiled floor on which she was struggling to get into a pair of fishnet hold-ups: I could see she was actually putting them on inside out. She was always a bit dopey in the mornings; it was a wonder she was ever on time. "Think the Doc's going to take away my methadone, though." She pulled a face at that. "Won't give a lot in one go, it's a pain to 'ave to pick it up all the fucking time." She looked very vulnerable still, even though she claimed to be off the heroin—she was skinny and looked like she needed a good meal. I felt sorry for her—she couldn't help it if she looked like a street urchin and hadn't been earning too well. Must have been more than when she was on street corners though.

"So it's helping then?" I offered. I had no idea about methadone, other than it was green and looked like toxic cough mixture, so Bella had said. The drug clinics gave it out as a substitute, on prescription, to help addicts get off heroin. Bella wasn't convinced, she said that more people died from methadone overdosing than from actual heroin; it was just a substitution of one drug for another.

Well, at least Ricky was off the street and getting a bit more settled in her bedsit, and she seemed happier than when she first came. She looked thin, but she was tidier and less pale and, on the whole, she was more together. Her wiry bleached hair was still in need of taming, but at least the roots were not showing any longer.

"Yeh, it's helping, I fink coz I moved from the estate. Thass 'elping too, not so much temptation, like there."

She rummaged in her canvas backpack for a lollipop, her stocking half on.

I looked down. "Darlin', you have that one on the wrong way."

"Ohhh, yeah, fanks," she gurgled, looking back at me bug-eyed, lolly in mouth.

"Want a lolly?" She thrust a packet at me. "Social worker gave um to me."

"No, thanks," I said, shaking my head. Just looking at her bony body made me feel lucky I had good parents—bugger, I felt guilty; I don't know why, I just did. I offered to get her a cup of tea; yes and five sugars was the reply. I ambled out into the kitchen and Suzie walked in. I smiled at her briefly but Suzie's eyes were hard. "Don't lend her any money—she'll just buy drugs with it," she said.

I hadn't planned to—I might look nice, but I'm not stupid.

When I went back into the bathroom with Ricky's tea, she asked me about giving head. Everybody knew it was a speciality of mine, and Ricky, keen to make more money, wanted a few tips. I wasn't really sure how to explain giving head. It just came naturally to me and gave me an over-whelming sense of power, and a thrill because it gives such pleasure. I start a blow-job by sucking down while pressing my tongue up against the shaft. Keeping the suction going, I slowly start to move up and down, before gently speeding up. Putting my hand around the base stops me from going too far and gagging if my head is suddenly pushed down further by an enthusiastic recipient! Looking up into his eyes as he watches you giving head is so horny—I always got a groan from the client when I did that.

To celebrate the house's fifth anniversary, Mrs. B had introduced hot and cold blow-jobs. They were a treat which could be requested by the regular clients...as if we weren't busy enough at that time! Ice cubes and hot tea were the main ingredients, although hot chocolate makes a great substitute, and a stickier option is ice cream and hot fudge sauce. Layla had taught me this one a few months earlier at the start of the mad Christmas rush when we were doing a Gemini together. She would alternate between a mouth full of hot tea then a mouth full of ice-cold water. It was extremely messy—we had to put towels down first to catch the liquid—but the result was much appreciated by the gentleman concerned. We didn't offer this service unless asked by a reg; it's such a big hassle to clean up and get done in a thirty-minute booking. I don't recommend it in the normal world either, even if you do have the time—unless he wants sex and she has a sweet tooth, that is.

I'm not sure Ricky listened properly to what I was saying to her, but I could only hope it would help her become popular with the clients. She was a lost kid and I really wanted her to sort herself out.

Sunday 8th March

All-day shift 10:30 a.m.–1 a.m.
17 x normal service + tips = £360
Minus £20 receptionist's fee
Total earned: £340

*T*he Publican was a funny guy—his wife had gone to Spain for a hen party and he came in three times that day to see me and then offered me a grand to stay the night at his. He had the money on him and was a genuinely nice guy. It was sooo tempting—not only was it *a lot* of money, but he was also a real laugh. In the end I didn't even take his number as I was too scared that Mrs. B would find out and I would be fired. On his way out he left a piece of paper with his details. I put it in my pocket and made a great show of chucking it straight in the bin, right in front of Tina, the house snitch, just in case it had been a set-up. I didn't think it could be, as he wasn't the type they normally used to trap girls—for a start, this guy smelled of money whereas the bosses' friends were all a bit rough around the edges. You can tell the sort, all talk, with scuffed shoes or worn cuffs. But you can never be too careful. Mr. B might have met him at the casino for all I knew and be doing him a favour.

The Publican told me he couldn't come in again as he was too scared his wife would find out—so that was that. Paranoia or what! Mind you, I could talk—my anxieties about people knowing what I did were spiralling out of control. My dress sense had gone down the tubes as I was trying to hide under shapeless black clothing. Meanwhile, socially, I was engineering even more ways to avoid ever going out. I began missing more and more classes and avoiding any situation where friends might try to set me up with suitable males. My mother wasn't helping, with her constant questions: "What are you working on at uni?" "What are you doing to earn money?" "Have you met anyone nice recently?" Real life as I had known it was slipping further from my grasp. I was worried that I felt so at home in the house and that I liked what I did for a living too much. Liking the money was one thing, but liking the job wasn't something you ever admitted to: it was a means to an end and that was it.

You shouldn't really like the work sex either, that would be an even worse admission—unless he was really cute, then that was deemed acceptable by the girls. Even if the guy had managed to rock my world, cute or not, it wouldn't have made much difference to me. I wouldn't have taken it further outside the house. My head was a bit messed up, but I knew I didn't want to end up in the same boat as some of the girls I'd met. I resolved not to cut myself off from the real world entirely.

Monday 9th March: The Scare

Evening shift 6 p.m.–1 a.m. (swapped my Tuesday shift with Layla)

4 x normal service + tips (including Asian guy) = £85

1½ hours with Chinese from Christmas who only gets Monday nights off + £10 tip = £70

Minus £10 receptionist's fee

Total earned: £145

*M*r. I Don't Care didn't seem remotely bothered when the condom broke, just shrugged and said there was no need to worry as he didn't have anything. How the hell would he know! He just showered and left. Ohhh, crap...In a weird way, it would have been more reassuring if he had been even slightly worried—at least if his sexual health mattered to him I could assume that he took care of himself. I was gutted—I'd just had my last bloody tests back and now I had to worry about having a whole new set done. I went for an examination and the nurse said

I'd probably know if there was anything wrong by the time I came back from Venice. If you are tested too soon it can often be a waste of time and show nothing, so I was advised to wait for a few weeks to see if anything materialized. God, I hated being in this situation, especially as I was so careful when it came to protecting myself. It was clear he was going to be fine, but that was no consolation to me. I was on top and, as I got off, my hand was around the condom as normal, just to make sure it didn't slip off. That was when I noticed the split around the top. I cleaned it up as I told him and popped in the shower after him. I felt shocked, but waved him off and ambled into the lounge and straight through to the bathroom to sit on the loo.

I have seen girls completely lose it, like Jane did, sitting on the bathroom floor, sobbing till a taxi is called to take them home. Some are quiet and just take the rest of the shift off, which is understandable. It rarely happened, but when it did, it was just awful. All sorts of horror runs through your head. Was it his fault? Did I put it on badly? Snag it with a nail? Is it really happening to me? What do I do if…if?

Glad I'm a bit more pragmatic than most. At least I was still on the pill, despite the fact I didn't need it for my personal sex life. It was supposedly helping balance my cycle still, and I had just finished my period, so pregnancy was the least of my worries. HIV and AIDS are the tip of a rather large, infectious iceberg and Hep is one of the things that worries me more than anything. My other anxiety was how the hell it had broken. I had been careful, hadn't I? Was the house using cheap condoms? The only real life lesson in the end is: must be more careful.

What's done is done; you can't change it. It's happened before and I was all right in the end. Had to be OK this time, too...Didn't I? God, I hoped so. Sometimes the reality of the job is hard to take and you realize just what you are risking. All I kept thinking was that if I had caught something I was going to need money, so leaving a shift and losing money was not the way to go. I decided there was no point getting myself stressed and all worked up about it till I knew for sure. No douching, as it could push anything there further up. Maybe more sex and the gravity of being on top would get it out. Deep breath: I would be fine...get back on the horse and all that. Only thing for it.

New Girl

One of the girls who had been working for a couple of weeks needed her hand holding while she went to the police station to report her violent husband. I was in early that morning and asked if she would like me to go with her. As I waited with her, I spotted one of my reg clients—a copper! He used to see one of the Russian girls when I wasn't there. (More about them later.) Now we knew how the police had gained their information—or was that just paranoia creeping in again? He had asked a lot of questions during our session, mostly about my age. After the Russian girl had been taken away, mysteriously he never came in again.

The latest new girl lived in the next town. She had been working in her own town, but too many people she knew had been coming into the house. She had to hide all the time, even from saying hello, and was losing so much work that the house wasn't happy. Also, a few of the girls were taking drugs, and she really didn't feel comfortable. I am not surprised—I would have hated it if drugs had been available at Mrs. B's house.

She liked the house straight away and was very eager. She did well—even did a kinky old couple who came in on her first day, who no one else, including myself, wanted to do. Tall, athletic, with long black hair, she was a smily, chirpy girl in her mid-twenties. Mrs. B had named her Alex.

Alex had obviously seen the other end of the scale when it came to houses and really appreciated her new environment. I knew that our house was good but, until she started to divulge, I didn't realize how good we had it. I had got used to my place of employment and had just thought that being well run and clean was the norm if you wanted to make a good profit, but obviously not.

"Well, of course you had to pay for your own rubbers," she was explaining to us as we sat around in the lounge, fascinated by her previous experiences.

"Yeah, I had to do that in the previous flat I worked in too," chipped in Sukey, in her broad council-estate drawl. "Dingy dark place with yellow walls and peeling wallpaper. Yehk."

"Threadbare carpet in the client rooms?" Alex countered back, like she had experienced that too.

"Yeah, what's with that? Must be in some 'How to decorate a whorehouse badly' book or something," Sukey threw back.

Alex nodded. "Our lounge in the other place was so small we nearly had to take it in turns for a seat, and the punters would come in and just pick one of us, no saying hello or anything, felt like a meat market. I hated it." She sipped her coffee and continued. "God, if those girls got drunk and only I got picked, I was in for hell. I would have to take my bag in the room with me to do a punter—I was more worried about the girls nicking from me than the guys!"

Sukey nodded, staring at Ricky, who was sitting on the edge of a chair sucking her lollipop nearby and said, "See I told you so, this is a good place. Grass is greener, my ass."

"Well, I was only finking, weren't I?" Ricky had been grumbling throughout the day about how she wanted more work and was asking around about other houses to work for as well as having her job at Mrs. B's. I guess my blow-job tips hadn't helped. Thinking about the dire conditions the other girls described kept us happy where we were. It was definitely the right choice to stay put.

Venice and Romance

The next day, at last, I was off on my trip to Venice. I hadn't slept the night before as I had been working and I knew I had to take the slow coach to France with the rest of the class in the morning. My night shift had ended at 3 a.m. I had taken yet another shower when I got home (this time a long one, not the rushed rubdown ones I have at work to keep me awake), I'd dressed, drunk coffee, and, picking up my small case by the door, headed out into the cold, across the road, to wait with the little huddled group of familiar staff and students for the 5 a.m. coach.

Excited as I was, I curled up on a seat and promptly fell asleep, only to wake with a start, having been patted on the shoulder by a fellow student. I had slept nearly all the way there.

After at least eighteen hours cramped up in the coach, we got out in a car park outside the city and proceeded to make our weary way over bridges to a small backstreet hotel. The tiny room I was sharing with the girls had bunkbeds and a small high window in the wall. It smelled damp but at least it was clean. That night I sat on my bunk and filled in various brightly coloured postcards I had picked up to send back home to my family and flatmates.

> *Hi girls*
> *Well, I eventually made it to Venice after hours on the coach. We arrived in the afternoon, around 1 p.m., and walked to our hotel, which is down a small street by the Grand Canal. By 3 we were out and about taking a vaporetto (waterbus) to San Marco square. Lots of architecture to see! I am having a great time! We all walked back through the narrow sidestreets, which are packed with shops that sell postcards, glass, lace, masks, beads, paintings, clothes, with small cafés and little restaurants here and there, on every corner and bridge you cross. The list goes on and on! Looking forward to the rest of the week, take care xxx*

Twenty of us were herded around by the staff the next day, and we didn't really feel free to roam till twilight, when we headed out for dinner at the local restaurant. I went back with the girls to our room afterwards. What with all that walking after the cramped captivity on the coach, I was in dire need of some good sleep.

On the fourth day, I was standing alone in the Peggy Guggenheim, the rest of my group having moved on to the other wing. My big *faux pas* of the day had been remarking to my fellow classmates that I thought the Jackson Pollock on the wall would "make great wrapping paper"...Well, it would—all that splattered and dribbled paint was very colourful! There was so much going on—shapes, textures, and colours—so I wasn't particularly freaked when, head tilted with one eye shut, staring through the window across the courtyard, I realized I definitely wasn't seeing things and that there was an eye blinking back at me. I have always been pretty observant and had already seen the shadow while looking at another piece on the wall. I had been taking the advice our art history lecturer had given us the week before. We should physically look at art in a different way...

The previous day I'd been doing just that and that was how I found myself being trampled on by a group of Japanese tourists! (I'm not kidding...I thought they only existed in the movies.) I had been lying on the floor looking up at the ceiling paintings in the Palazzo Ducale (Doge's Palace). Our group had moved on to another room—my friends had been too embarrassed to join me on the floor. I had been staring up, noting the characters dancing before me, when the stampede occurred. Everyone in the group was looking up as they walked, and no one noticed me lying there until I squealed. A hand suddenly came from nowhere and helped me up to my feet. It belonged to a gentleman in his fifties, probably old enough to be my father, but what the hell, he was a nice chap. I said thank you and dusted myself off...it was like I had been trampled by a herd of elephants! I found out that he was an American there on business, taking the afternoon off from meetings to see the sights. We chatted on the way around the palace, following my group as we toured the ancient prison where the infamous Casanova had been held for several years before making his escape.

I asked him if he had seen the Peggy Guggenheim, as we were to spend tomorrow morning there. No, he hadn't been there yet. It was on his list of places to visit, though, maybe he would see me there. And just like that, we had gone our separate ways.

It was there, with one eye shut, head tilted, staring into space, that I heard him whisper "Boo" in my ear. That startled me. He was leaving in the morning and asked me if I would keep him company over dinner that night, if I could slip away from the rabble? I said I didn't think that was such a good idea as I didn't really know him at all, so I invited him to join our group at the restaurant that night.

When he arrived that evening, he gave me a large, wrapped package, saying that he had seen it that afternoon in a shop window on the walk back to his hotel and on impulse had bought it for me. It was a gorgeous eye mask with gold trim and a plume of long black feathers with a slight green shimmer at the top. I thanked him profusely and then we sat down, just off from the main table, and talked for ages. He paid for my meal, we swapped numbers, and I left with the last few girls as he sat there finishing his drink. That wasn't the last I saw of him, I am glad to say. He was pleasant, polite, and I just felt comfortable in his company. I always have been a sucker for a geeky American gent—in fact, any intellectual, remotely geeky guy was a real turn-on. My ideal man would have the body of a cave man and the mind of an accountant. Don't worry: I really don't understand it either...

Venice was magical, it was fabulous to see the original art after looking at all those badly reproduced pictures in books. There really is no substitute for the real thing, and it was well worth all the hard work that went into saving up. It was a double whammy to meet someone nice in a city notorious for romance.

The man I had met there came to London for work soon after I returned from Venice, so I drove up to see him. I met him at his hotel, a plush, exclusive little place with exceptionally attentive staff who made me feel slightly on edge—given that he was quite a lot older than me and I looked really young for my age, we must have looked a little strange together. As we sat at dinner I told him what I did to keep me afloat as a student. I think he had probably guessed as much from various snippets. He did not seem fazed at all. I stayed the night at his hotel; he was an easy-going guy I felt comfortable with, not handsome but not ugly either. At least he knew the score and was quite happy to just have a fling. We played around a bit, but he was tired and promptly fell asleep...not surprising really, as we had chatted a lot about his work and he had consumed a large bottle of red wine with dinner. I was a bit frustrated, staying awake most of the night watching the box as I was too wired to sleep; also, he snored. The flashing screen didn't disturb him in the slightest, but I made a note to myself that, if there was to be a next time, I would bring a good book. I tried not to ponder on the fact that my test results were due back soon, especially in the dead of night when I was alone with my thoughts. I left in the morning after a room-service breakfast and a long, hot shower. He even gave me £100 for petrol.

He mentioned other planned business trips which meant he would be around and then said he would love to take me to Paris for the weekend, sight-seeing and shopping...Sex and shopping with someone else's money—what a perfect scenario! I love it when a plan comes together!

We kept in touch on the phone—I didn't want him forgetting me, did I? He was going to be over at the end of June for a meeting in Bonn. Did I want to meet up in Paris for the weekend? He would leave a ticket at the airport for me to collect. Bingo! He would meet me at the airport the other end and whisk me off. Double bingo!

Excitement about Paris was compounded by the nurse confirming that there wasn't any evidence down below to suggest I had anything immediate to feel anxious about, so I needn't worry about coming in for three months unless I felt ill. I could get on with life and worry about it in twelve weeks. Fine by me. I decided to get back to the house and keep my mind off it.

Sunday 29th March:
Back to Work

All-day shift 10:30 a.m.–1 a.m.

11 x normal service + tips (including The Son or Prop No.3) =
£255

Minus £20 receptionist's fee

Total earned: £235

*B*ack at work I didn't seem to attract any particular age group. The Son, a prop in the Colts rugby team, was one of the more memorable young ones. He must have been all of eighteen...bless. Nervous and scared, he had picked me because I looked friendly. That generally seemed to be the main reason I was picked. Anyway, I walked into the room and found him wrapped in his towel, face down on the bed. I took off my robe and sat next to him. Starting the massage, we chatted as I rubbed him down. He had a nice compact body—tight muscles that needed relaxing—give him a few more years and he would be a strapping lad. I was desperate to flip him over and whip off the towel that was snugly wrapping his hips. I stood up and took off my underwear as he turned over, lying there staring up at me. I reached out and started to pull at the towel. He did nothing to stop me, his hand coming up to stroke my side as I wrested the towel off him, freeing his erection. I knelt on the bed as he sat up to stroke my breasts, his hand shaking. I could swear he was a virgin! I decided to take it slower than normal. I lay down and let him stroke me until he stopped shaking, all the while getting more and more excited. I eased up and took long, slow sucks at his warm cock. Lying there, he watched my progress, moaning till I pulled away, and then he was on me. Lifting my hips beneath him, I received him in shuddering spurts. He lasted longer than I thought he would before he came and fell in a sweaty heap in my arms. I stroked him till he calmed down, rolled him over, and cleaned him off, ushering him into the shower as I tidied the rumpled bed.

His father, in his fifties, came in on my next shift, having overheard his son talking to his mate about what a good time he'd had. He had heard my name and where I worked and had decided to come in to see what all the fuss was about! It goes without saying that the father was the better screw. But what the boy lacked in experience he made up for with sheer enthusiasm. The father asked me not to say anything to his boy if he should come in again. I saw the boy again a few times after that and also acquired two of his friends as clients. I don't mind younger men, but they are sooo much trouble to train properly; it's an effort to slow them down and get them to take it easy—but it's the only way to make sure there is something in it for you!

Give me a man over at least twenty-eight any day. They shouldn't need telling where everything is at that age. I suppose I'm a lazy screw at heart. The older they are, the better. Sounds strange, but I am not kidding. The oldest guy I have ever dated was seventy. Thank god for Viagra is all I can say.

Footloose and Fancy
at a Fee

The four thirteen- and fourteen-year-old girls who turned up at the front door one morning were a surprise. Cebell wasn't in yet. Mr. B was there, as he had opened up that morning. A new girl, Kirsty, was also there but was showering ready for her next shift. Even if she had been available to talk to them, being new herself she didn't know much anyway. I was in early, already dressed in my uniform and my long red satin robe, ready to catch the morning rush.

They kept on ringing the bell. Mr. B didn't want to answer it—thought it would be inappropriate if he answered. He said to ignore them. But they just stood there; through the camera we could see them outside on the step. I decided to go and see what was up before they scared off any early morning clients or girls.

Mr. B came with me and stood at the top of the stairs in case I needed any help. I headed slowly down the steps, taking a deep breath. Crap. I opened the door a few inches.

They'd looked young on the camera and, in real life, they looked even younger.

"Can I help you?"

"Yes," the ringleader piped up, standing there in a track-suit, tightly permed hair scraped back in a pony-tail and big loopy gold earrings hanging from her ears. She said she had a sister who had worked here in the past and thought it would be a great way to earn loads of money. They explained what they knew. "How old do you have to be?" she asked me. I looked at them in shock. They were so young, yet they seemed to know all about what went on.

"Can we come in and chat?" whispered a darker-haired girl.

"I don't think that would be a good idea...You have to be over eighteen to work here," I said, wide-eyed. A girl standing behind asked, "Can you pick the good-looking guys to see?"

"No." I emphasized that, mostly, they were old, fat, and smelly. I lied, and added for good measure that, at night, if they had been drinking, things could be a bit rough. (Sorry, guys!) I wasn't going to make this job sound glamorous. Because it's not.

"So what can you do to make more money here?" the pony-tailed ringleader asked. I don't think anything I said was going to put that one off—she was far too interested. So I changed tack and said that, if they wanted to make more money, what they really needed to do was continue their schooling. I explained that the smarter girls made more money, as quite often the rich guys liked to chat as well as everything else—the more stuff you knew and the more you could chat, the bigger the tips. It was all about making the punter feel relaxed and helping the whole thing feel as "normal" as possible.

They nodded and looked as if they had taken it in. Hell...I hoped they stayed in school and didn't end up on the street as, judging by what I saw, that was the only place at their age they would have been able to work. They would be too young to work in a safe house...jail-bait, the lot of them. Their eagerness really disturbed me.

I told them as nicely as I could that a group of people on our doorstep didn't help business and scared customers away. Tightly wrapped in my robe, I was astonished at their candour. I stood half behind the door as I waved them goodbye.

I was shell-shocked when I went to sit down in the kitchen. It is the only time I have known Mr. B put the kettle on for a cuppa. He didn't actually make the tea but said, "Thanks for that," and squeezed me on the shoulder, smiling as he passed to let another girl in. I think that still waiting to know for sure about the outcome of my latest scare was affecting my reaction to simple things, but those girls really haunted me. They had no idea what they could be getting themselves into and, more worrying still, it struck me that the ringleader couldn't have cared less anyway.

I made the tea and waited for the new girl, Kirsty, to come out of the bathroom so I could introduce her to the mousse-can demo—otherwise known as the house condom-rolling test. As Carry wasn't in, I felt it was up to me to show her the ropes. Kirsty looked embarrassed and was all fingers and thumbs. Never mind—maybe she would be better at the chit-chat? As I'd said to the girls on the doorstep of the house, I realized that being educated, even a little bit, really did help. No matter how sexually experienced you were, chat always came in handy. In this profession, chat is so important to break the ice, so studying a few "boy" subjects was a very good idea, from horseracing to rugby and, of course, football. Motor GP, Formula One—anything that included motor sports really. Most loved it when I told them I could change a tyre in fifteen minutes flat without breaking a nail. Wine and whisky, cigars and gambling of any sort were a real winner too. Mr. B was no exception—he loved his whisky and gambling as well. Making sure his crystal whisky glass was washed up at the end of the night, sparkling clean, and put away, would always put me in his good books!

Having a broad knowledge of men's hobbies is something I recommended to all the new girls—I've still got to work on my chess and my understanding of cricket, though! Kirsty gazed at me with a vacant look in her eyes. I had a feeling she might not make it. I was right—she quit that evening.

Friday 17th April

All-day shift 10:30 a.m.–1 a.m.
15 x normal service + tips (including Doctor Dickhead – £5
tip) = £350
Minus £20 receptionist's fee
Total earned: £330

"Doctor Dickhead" was an Indian guy in his late forties. Wore gloves and insisted on trying to wear two rubbers till I explained that two would only rub against each other and split (titbit from our sex therapist, Carry). I explained that the polymers—or some such—don't like the friction and disintegrate in the process, therefore two are more likely to split than one. For a doctor—and he had to be a doctor, even though he denied it—he was not very clued up. Is it any wonder so many of us girls will only have female doctors? Anyhow, Doctor Dickhead would make me shower in front of him to make sure I "did it properly." Arrogant bastard! I wouldn't have minded if it was a role-play sort of thing, but he meant it!

I was only then allowed to join him on the sofa and sit in a towel. I eventually got him to follow me on to the bed and he started stabbing me with rough fingers and manhandling me with heavy hands. Even when I asked him to be more gentle, he carried on the same way as before, just more slowly, and then he asked if he was any good! Hmm, how do you answer that *and* keep your client happy?

He seemed to think that he had the magic touch.

"Yeah, right, tell that to Carry, who refuses even to say hello to you in the waiting room let alone see you, because you're such a twat" is what I really wanted to say, but when a girl needs money...It's not like screwing for a living is all fun and games: at least 80 percent of the time it's no fun at all, but I don't like to dwell on that for too long, as it can bring you down. And the 20 percent fun is the bit that counts!

He always gave me a £5 tip at the end, like it was something special. He really was vile—so much so that the last time he saw me, I snapped. With the thought of the bruises that were about to appear, I'd had enough and (after he gave me the tip) I told him he was a bit rough.

He stormed out in a huff and I never saw him again. Think he came back and saw other new girls. Thank goodness for that, otherwise I was seriously contemplating paying the house from my own pocket just to ensure I didn't have to see him! I remember feeling sorry for his poor wife if she had to endure his rough handling, not to mention his patients if he examined them as roughly.

How do you define a crap shag? Well, a few ways actually. The pokey-pokey, stabby-stabby finger doesn't help and neither does continuous pumping away in the same position till you're red-raw. Tongue in ear, face slobbering, painful pinning to the bed, the hand on the back of your head shoving a cock down your throat and making you gag. Do I really have to say any more? Let's just say that most men who came to the house were rubbish. For goodness sake, civilians, will you please train your men properly? Otherwise they end up at our door. A good lay is becoming a rare commodity.

I have seen enough male doctors as clients by now to freak me out should I need to see one. I have "female doctor only" on my notes now, especially for gynaecologists. I had a male one once who told me very matter-of-factly, "This won't hurt." I had to ask him how he knew, as he was a man.

"No one has complained before," he countered, looking at me blankly.

Yes, like I haven't heard that one before!

Sunday 19th April

All-day shift 10:30 a.m.–1 a.m.
13 x normal service + tips = £275
Minus £20 receptionist's fee
Total earned: £255

*H*ans the German was living in this country and working as a photographer. Not one of us in the kinky queue liked saying hello to him. Some girls refused to see him at all (Layla point blank), and I couldn't blame them really; he was a nasty piece of work. He wanted you on your knees from the door crawling in to kiss his feet, wanted his balls and anus licked, wanted total submission, and was bloody rude when you declined for health reasons. He wanted you kneeling at his feet, hands behind your back, begging to let you lick him. Then he would bend you over his knee and shove his fingers up you, saying that if you asked nicely he might grant you access to his cock and "fuck your sorry little pussy, you dirty little bitch." After making me crawl around on the floor in his direction, I would suck the rubber on (not that he liked wearing a rubber) and he would bend me over the bed, kick my legs apart, prise my cheeks apart, and shove his way in, pounding away, all the time calling me a dirty little whore in need of a thorough fucking to show me what a real man was like! Give me a break—with that attitude, is it any wonder he had to visit the house!

I saw him quite a few times as no one else would put up with his shit. I had heard it all before, so it didn't bother me as much as most and it wasn't as if he was a paedophile, like some I had to deal with. They *were* harder to deal with—if only by a small margin.

It wasn't until he went with a new girl and she scared him off that we got rid of him...Lana, who just happened to be a photographer too (and a damn good one at that), had been talking to him about cameras as she started the massage. Things got a little heated, as it turned out she had a better camera, knew more about photography than he did, and wouldn't put up with his stupid demands (later on in the massage he tried to force her to lick his ass after she had said no). There was a lot of shouting and she threw him out, telling him he was a "disgusting prick" and not to come back!

Mrs. B wasn't too happy, but Lana got a round of applause from us girls, although she only worked a couple more shifts after that, saying she couldn't put up with all the pricks. Go, girl!

Night out with the Boss

Layla, Sanita, and I were closer to Mr. and Mrs. B than the other girls. We were all good earners and, despite the fact that I say so myself, we were all pretty and having us around made them look good in front of their friends. On a few occasions we would be asked to go out to dinner with them and their guests. Just dinner, mind, nothing extra, Mrs. B said; it was just a way of saying thank you for all our hard work. We weren't stupid, but hey, a free meal in a nice restaurant is never to be turned down. The only place we didn't go was the casino as, for some reason, it was an unwritten rule that we weren't allowed—that was the domain of Mr. Boss and his cronies.

Mr. B's birthday was one of those occasions when they took us out. They hired the whole of a small local Italian restaurant and set up the tables in a long line. Having been invited, it felt rude not to accept; we were treating it as some quality catch-up time, and an opportunity to be in the good books was always a bonus too. So we clubbed together and bought him the biggest big bottle of his favourite tipple we could find as a gift. It was a good night out in the end but a little boring, as I got stuck with a pervy old guy who was writing a parlour review book. He popped up at the house every now and then. The house would give him freebies (half an hour with a girl) in return for a good review. The house would give the girl £30 as compensation to do a good job. Poor Layla had tickled his fancy a couple of months back when they had spent time arguing about politics. A blow-job was all he got out of it as he came too fast in the end. But £30 was better than nothing as far as Layla was concerned.

Layla couldn't stand his "pompous ass" and refused to see him again, but he still seemed to like her and gave her a 5-star review (which was still in his book for many years after she left the house), so there I was, stuck having to keep Mr. No Personality Pervert occupied, as Layla refused to speak to him. Sanita found it highly amusing and kept laughing across the table—even more so when he fell asleep face down in his dessert! We left him there, gurgling in his fruit salad. All three of us said our goodbyes and got a cab home, Sanita giggling and slightly tipsy.

Back at the house, girls continued to come and go, some of whom I never met, as they left almost as soon as they had started, but the two Russian girls worked out well. They were nice to the clients and spoke many languages, including English, which was an asset to the house. Both were of medium build: Dacha had the bigger chest and was the more outspoken of the two; Rachel was the observant listener, with brown eyes and mid-shoulder brown hair, compared to Dacha's straggly black hair and lighter hazel eyes. They kept to themselves but were friendly in general and gave the customers no reason to complain. They had been at the house for about three months when there was another police raid. It just happened to be on the day when both girls were working. Somehow the police had found out they were in the country illegally and had turned up to arrest and deport them. From what I heard from another girl who had been there at the time, about ten officers turned up and ushered them away without checking the other girls' ID or taking names. They obviously knew who they wanted, and Mrs. B hadn't interfered. She had had no idea that they were illegal immigrants, and she was sad to see them leave. She never heard from them again and just supposed they had been sent back to Russia.

I was always sad to see good girls go, especially when they had come here to earn money and change their circumstances. Part of me felt guilty that all I had to worry about was an all-expenses-paid trip to the city of love with my minted American...

Tuesday 28th April

All-day shift 10:30 a.m.–1 a.m.
11 x normal service + tips = £250
Minus £20 receptionist's fee
Total earned: £230 (slow all day, everyone was whingeing about it)

I want 'im...'e's mine!...'e's mine, 'e's mine, 'e's mine." I heard the voice coming from the lounge. The buzzer had just gone. I had shown a client to the back door and then walked around the corner to see Fifi bouncing on her chair chanting, "'e's mine." Fifi was a French nymphomaniac, a gangly, Goth-looking girl. She was the most unlikely girl in the world ever to be called Fifi. I think she chose her own name, as I can't see Mrs. B choosing it—the names *she* picked suited each girl down to a T; this one was more Morticia than bloody Fifi.

She rarely got picked: she wore too much eyeliner and I think it scared off the clients. If it had been a particularly quiet day for her, it wasn't unusual for her to be sitting waiting for the next man to ring the bell and get her all excited. Now, we all made moves to go out and say our hellos. Fifi shot me a look like she had been smacked in the face with a wet Durex. She hated the hello line-up competition. I really didn't need a sulking Fifi all day. Fifi went and said hello first, as I quickly dumped my rubbish and got in the queue behind the rest. I walked to the doorway and saw a timid old guy sitting there. "Hello, I am Fifi, plllleasure to meet you!" I purred, and went and sat down in the lounge. That should do it.

Fifi sat in a huff—till, "Fifi you're up," was called by the receptionist and put an automatic smile on her face. Well, that should shut her up, fingers crossed he really had picked her and wouldn't send her back to get me or I would be in for it. After twenty-five minutes she bounded in and I gave her a coffee as she liked it. Phew, one happy nympho.

Thankfully, not all the girls were touchy; in fact, the best ones were those with a sense of humour, like Bella. She was the portly, motherly Domme with shiny boots who had educated me about the condom when I first started. She was a relaxed and easygoing lady but, beneath it all, lay a will of iron. There wasn't that much work for her and she left later in the summer, but in the short time I worked with her, she opened my eyes to another world.

Credit to the Dommes of this world: it takes a strong person to deal with all the accompanying crap, as it leaves you feeling mentally drained, much more so than straight sex ever can. Contrary to popular opinion, being a Domme doesn't mean just shouting at a guy and beating him stupid. You need creativity, imagination, and sheer grit to control a situation.

I saw this firsthand when I walked in and saw a guy huddled in the corner, with Bella towering over him.

"Come in," she had boomed when I knocked at the door of the small room. Two sets of eyes stared at me when I opened the door.

I addressed Bella. "Do you mind if I sit in here to read? It's getting a bit noisy out there. The girls are singing to a music video," I explained.

"Sure...have a seat." She winked at me.

We'd arranged this earlier. Her regular loved to be humiliated in front of someone else and I had agreed to sit in. If the receptionist needed me to say hello, she would knock.

"How dare you presume yourself worthy of her attention," she shouted at the man, kicking the wide-eyed, naked lump on the floor. I sat on the sofa, crossed my legs and watched. "You dog shit. Look up at my radiant cunt. Gaze up and worship it, you piece of shit...Isn't it the most gorgeous thing you have ever seen? If you had the choice between licking my delicious cunt, or running to your mummy, you show me which you'd choose...Yeah, that's right, lick it. Lick my heavenly cunt, you worm, prettier lips than your ugly bitch mother [laughing]...Yeah, umm, that's right, lick softly, that's right, get your tongue right in. If you say please it will be my arsehole next. Go on, kiss my feet and beg, little boy."

The knock on the door fifteen minutes later was from Louise. I left the magnificent Bella there, the poor creature prostrated under her feet, begging for queening. I had always wondered what that word meant! Basically, it means a Domme's subject was her throne, and she would sit on his face as he squirmed under the weight and mumbled happy noises of appreciation. At the same time, she swatted his dick with a fly swat, one of those plastic ones, in a baby-blue colour. Swish...swish...whack...yelp! That was the last thing I heard as I closed the door behind me.

Work Obsession

He had never voiced his opinion. You see, I know him very well. That's why today, as a treat, I headed down to the fancy-dress shop, leaving a message on his pager to turn up at my flat at 9 p.m. sharp. He will turn up on time—he always does. At 8:59 p.m. I leave the front door ajar. I hear his steps—you can't miss them—the thuds get louder, the door creaks open, and he enters the darkly lit hall. He ventures inside, calling my name. I emerge from behind the door, slamming it closed with a bang and flicking on the light. He's about to turn as I place the cold metal barrel of my gun against the base of his skull. He holds his breath. "Don't even think about it, boy," I murmur in his ear. He slowly breathes out, he knows it's me...the game has started!

"But..." he utters.

"Shut up, face the wall, hands above your head, legs apart. Well, well, what have I got here—a burglar, breaking and entering...tut...tut..." I frisk him with a gloved hand, the other on the metal at the base of his head. I put my roaming hand over his crotch. He is getting slightly hard. I can feel it springing into life.

I whisper in his ear, "Who is being a bad boy then...I can't hear you," pushing the barrel at his head and increasing the pressure. "When I speak, you are to answer 'Yes, ma'am' or 'No, ma'am.' Do you understand?"

"Yes, ma'am," he answers timidly.

"Good boy. Now, hands on your head and walk." Rather sternly I direct him to a chair in the middle of the bedroom. The chair faces away from the bed but the mirror in the corner shows a glimpse of the large bed lightly draped in black satin behind. "Sit." He eases into the chair, hands by his side. I slap him on the side of the head. "Did I tell you to take your hands off your head?" (His hands return to his head.) "Did I?"

"No, ma'am." He hangs his head but glances at my reflection in the mirror.

I can see from the glint of a grin that he likes the police uniform. My hair is pinned up severely, the tight little white shirt divided with a black-and-white-checked cravat, the miniscule black skirt, stockings, and black stiletto boots. "Put your hands behind you." I cuff his hands behind the chair, clicking each cuff shut but not too tight. Placing the toy gun in the back of the waistband of my skirt, I walk around the chair to face him. He looks up at me with glazed eyes. "I can see I have your attention now." I place my hand on his shoulder and my booted foot in his groin, bearing down as I do so.

I awoke sweating, damp, bolt upright! It was the night after I had witnessed the submission of Bella's punter. I don't normally remember my dreams, but this one was so vivid I sat up in bed with the bedside lamp on and wrote it down in my sketchpad, which I keep by the side of my bed.

Bella wasn't the only one to deal with the weird and wonderful; we all had our own share to deal with. The men came from all walks of life and were generally pretty average-looking; most were a straight suck and a fuck, but lurking among them would be the dark ones, those who liked to push the boundaries. I was rarely chosen by them, as my image was that of a happy-go-lucky girl rather than the sterner hand they required. This was fine by me. I didn't have the experience to deal with them anyway: that would come with practice. Meanwhile, I would have to make do with dreaming about it!

Sunday 17th May

All-day shift 10:30 a.m.–1 a.m.
11 x normal service + tips = £235
Minus £20 receptionist's fee
Total earned: £215

I met a gentleman the girls had christened Baby Girl. On first hearing the name and being sent to him, I assumed he had picked me as I looked young, but the reality was certainly a surprise.

Baby Girl is probably one of the most way-out-there clients I've ever had to deal with, then or now. He was a respectable-looking bloke in a grey suit, a bit shy and quiet. The surprise was the layers of pink he loved to wear under his suit. He accessorized the outfit with a child's plastic beaded bracelet hidden underneath the cuff of his lawyer's shirt. A heavy lump in pink frilly underpants was the sight that greeted me when I entered the Ballroom. Softly spoken, he sat on my knee while I brushed his hair, and he explained in a squeaky voice what he wanted. The routine was always the same: I would disappear on an errand, come back into the room, with a glass of iced water, for example, to "catch" him standing there kitted out in a pink ruffled blouse, pink skirt, and pink frilly socks, complete with small pigtails and badly applied make-up. He had brought the entire outfit in with him, hidden in a bulky holdall. "Bad girl," I would have to scold, "with Mummy's lipstick all over you, make-up everywhere!" I would then explain that he needed to be punished. I would stretch him out over my knee, pulling up the skirt and pulling down the panties around his ankles in one go. I would then rub in baby oil and proceed to spank him with a ruler, smacking hard, with long, sweeping strokes, across his glistening pink rump, leaving red raw welts across his backside, a warm, fiery glow. For the finishing touch, I plucked an ice cube from my glass of water and applied it to his backside in order to help take down the swelling. The shock of the ice cube against his skin would cause him promptly to slide to the floor, wanking as he went; thumb in mouth he would stay seated cross-legged at my feet as I stroked his hair, him merrily filling the underwear around his ankles with spunk. Before he left he would neatly fold the knickers and put them in his coat pocket for safekeeping, informing me that it would remind him of what a naughty little girl he had been!

I grew fond of him; he was sweet in a weird sort of way.

The Kinky Confession...

*I*t soon became clear that there was discontent brewing back at the camp. Business had been a bit slow. I think we were all hoping it was just the time of year, but while I was lucky and had my regulars, most of the girls weren't in such a fortunate position. Unlike some of the newer girls, I couldn't be accused of taking money from others by stealing their clients. I had my set list of regs and it didn't interfere with anyone else's earning potential.

My real anxiety was waiting for my test results. I felt OK, but that didn't really mean much, I could still have caught something nasty. I began to really stress—what if I'd passed it on to someone already? As a distraction, I started throwing myself into my art. My work was becoming very dark, just like my clothing. Simon was worried—he started commenting on how quiet I was, how I was retreating into myself. Hardly anybody else had noticed: I had pulled away from socializing to such an extent that I was barely talking to anyone in class any more—that is, if I turned up at all. I was doing all my art projects on my own in my room and the only human contact I had was when I was at home with Layla and Sanita or when I was on duty at the house.

I was such a loner that it was hard to remember how it happened, how I came to tell Simon where I worked. He had a habit of smoking pot in his room, covering up the fire alarm and putting towels around the door to stop the smoke from escaping, but if I was in the hazy room with him I would get terribly light-headed and have to stand by the open window to keep my head clear. I had gone round to his room to get some notes from the lecture I had missed the week before and for a good old natter, as I had a feeling he wanted to talk. I didn't realize it was me he wanted to talk about.

"OK, chuck, what's going on? Come on, confess—you're up to something. What are you on? Coke?"

"What?!"

"You're tired, withdrawn, looking a bit thin, runny nose, and wearing baggy clothing like you have something to hide." He looked up from his Rizlas and stared me straight in the eye. "Come on, fess up."

"Do people really think I'm a cokehead?" I was all wide-eyed and worried.

"No," he said, getting back to the mission at hand.

"Phew," I sighed.

"No," he said again. "Natasha thinks you're on speed and wonders why you haven't come to her, as she has a good doc who can get you 'diet pills' like hers; Sebastian thinks you're a secret drinker and says you should really come to an AA meeting with him." He huffed, lighting up. "I...am just wondering where you get your coke from and can you hook me up?"

Shit, they think I am twatted up—not good at all. Too many shifts and not enough sleep and working through the cold Sanita had lovingly passed to me hadn't helped recently. I knew I didn't look great and that a lot of the people he knew did drugs, but I would rather tell him what I was up to than have him think I was a junkie. How mortifying that people should think I was dependent like that.

"Ha, ha, very funny," I smirked, but too late—he was sharp and had caught my wan expression.

"I'm not laughing, girl, I'm worried about you. I can see the signs, you know—you're behaving just like I did before I came out, afraid of being persecuted, and paranoid. I still have problems telling people I'm gay even now."

That was true. He would only mention his "partner" in passing and generally didn't talk to many people if he could help it.

"Simon, I hate to say this, but you don't have to tell anyone, we all know." I looked at him sympathetically and put my hand on his knee.

"Really!" It was his turn to go pale. "Shit, how?"

"Not stereotyping or anything, but all the pink you wear and the picture of your poodle in your wallet kinda give you away."

It was starting to tick over in my head what people might think of me if they thought that of him. Bugger—no wonder people thought I was on something. All my paranoia about being caught out was just how one of my junkie cousins acted. Well, at least they didn't think I was a prostitute; that was some consolation. I suppose I would have needed PVC boots and a mini-skirt for them to think that...

"You're right, that might give it away, yep," Simon pondered, rocking on his chair at his desk. "But *you're* not gay, as there is no way you'd have turned down Natasha, so it's got to be drugs."

Damn, he was still on a roll. All the smoke was making me dizzy so I moved over to the window and opened it.

"No, not drugs. I work in the sauna down the road. I'm just a bit tired at the moment and having flu last week didn't help."

He looked up. "Ah, the brothel down the road? You OK? They aren't forcing you to do stuff, are they?"

I looked him square in the eye. "Since when can anyone force me to do anything? I thought you knew me?" I breathed in the fresh air and turned to face him again. He was taking it better than I thought.

"Well, as long as you're OK. Just promise me you're using rubber and, for fuck's sake, don't do porn!"

I smirked at that. "Porn doesn't pay enough and isn't safe anyway." He nodded and came over to give me a big hug.

I felt like a huge weight had been lifted from my shoulders. I had a civilian in my corner. OK, a pot-smoking gay one, but still one of the saner members of the gang. Simon wasn't vindictive and wouldn't hurt anyone. I hugged him back. This was definitely damage control: he would be very good at keeping the others off my case and would displace any rumours that popped up.

"Don't worry—I won't tell anyone you're gay," I whispered in his ear.

He giggled. "Think the cat's out of the bag on that one, hun! Anyway, here are the notes." He handed me a big folder crammed full of neatly written notes.

"OK, thanks. Will get them back to you, chat later, got to dash." I removed the damp towels from around the door and escaped the cloud-filled room, closing the door behind me.

"Talk dirty to me" was the request I hated the most. It was hard to do the first time. My mind would draw a blank and, if asked in the middle of sex, it would totally break my concentration. I'd freeze and my heart would sink. I just didn't know what to say. What the hell do you say? I found that watching house porn helped to prepare me for situations like this, but it took months of working at the house to feel easy about it and not giggle at the "Come on, then, boy, fuck me harder! Faster!" and all the other lines that came to mind. It helped to say them over and over again out loud, sometimes to the mirror. I stopped feeling embarrassed, but it took longer to master than any other technique I learned.

On a par with talking dirty was the age-old question: "What's the kinkiest thing you have ever done?" Now, would that be what a "normal" person would call kinky? That question always stumps me. I don't mean to sound blasé but, when you have done so many weird and wonderful things, what is the definition of kinky? In my world, even the outrageous stuff seems pretty normal after a while!

Tell me. Is being handcuffed to a boat rail kinkier than spanking a lawyer with a ruler when he's dressed in pink, frilly girl's knickers? Is a lesbian show kinkier than buggering a man with a strap-on? What about dressing in rubber from head to foot? Or an orgy? The list is endless, so what's the kinkiest thing I've ever done? Answers on a postcard would be much appreciated.

Talking about kinky, Bella wanted us to try out a new paddle on her. Huh?...Hang on—she's a Domme right? I must have misheard—me and my smutty mind...She had announced this to a stunned group of girls. "Never hit, spank, or cane someone unless you know what it feels like—that way, you know how hard to go." I was intrigued, so we tried out the stiff, black, shiny paddle in the bathroom. I couldn't see what all the fuss was about; to me it just hurt. We were careful to only hit gently, in an upward motion, as Bella explained it caused less damage. It wouldn't pull the skin down so wouldn't tear and bruise as much, but it would sting, which was the required element. As we weren't into it and Mrs. B would have gone ballistic if we had got bruises, we only gave a few soft strokes using Bella's different implements. It was hilarious, and Paris found it particularly amusing, standing giggling in the doorway. It was all broken up by the door bell, and we trotted off to say a really kinky hello, Bella waving the paddle and nearly scaring the wits out of the sixty-year-old guy who was sitting there. He took ages to choose and asked to see us all again—minus the "black scary lady with the whip." He made his mind up and picked Kerry, the "curly-haired blonde with the big earrings." It wasn't unusual for guys to forget our names, especially if you had a day when Carry, Kerry, and Sherry were working the same shift. No wonder they got confused!

I turned up one morning to cover a shift for Kerry. I wasn't supposed to be working, but I swapped because she had had a call from her babysitter and needed to change her shift. I'd just come up from a room when I was greeted by lots of yelling in the lounge. It wasn't unusual for Paris to be on a rant but I could tell from Mrs. B's red, angry face that something was really wrong. Paris had just been fired for stealing—in fact, she had been helping herself for weeks. News had been filtering through that she was setting up a new sauna down the coast. It was only noticed when she was seen by the receptionist trying to shove two fluffy shower mats into her already overstuffed holdall while the other girls were saying their kinky hello. That was the day the whole house had being doing a cranberry-juice detox day, which involved drinking litres of juice to flush out toxins. We were all (including the receptionist) running to the loo every five minutes. Paris had been caught red-handed after popping to the loo while she thought everyone would be distracted. She had had a good thing going until she was caught. Now, she flounced off, her emptied bag thrown out the back door as Mrs. B shouted after her. After she left, we discovered that she had also been signing on the dole under various names. We never saw her after that but heard she opened a sauna, that it was doing OK, and that she had bought a bigger car, so she must have landed on her feet.

Sunday 10th May

All-day shift 10:30 a.m.–1 a.m.
9 x normal service (including Mr. Golden Shower) = £180
Minus £20 receptionist's fee
Total earned: £160

In this game, there's no chance of slack muscles. My muscles down below got stronger with constant use, and there was one reg in particular who benefited from that very firm muscle—Mr. Golden Shower.

Watersports was not something that every girl in the house would do; this little activity is an acquired taste. I have to admit, I'm not too keen myself, but hey...if a guy gets turned on by me peeing on him, I don't mind obliging. As long as he doesn't want to piss on me, that's fine.

Quickly guzzling two pints of warm water before starting really helped, and there was a water cooler in every room if you needed any more help. Placing him back against the wall in the shower, I would stand over my Golden Boy, wiggling as I peed. He also liked being put in a bath of warm water, as I could then shower him from head to foot. He loved to gargle with the warm stuff too, as well as me showering his face in long, hot squirts. But, most of all, he liked just to stare up at my golden snatch as I sprinkled and wank off. It's a messy business, and he was a thoroughly dirty boy by the time I had finished with him.

Tuesday 9th June

All-day shift 10:30 a.m.–1 a.m. (sick cover)
8 x normal service = £160
Double Decker, after Tina = £20
No receptionist's fee
Total earned: £180

I really like foot-worshippers. It's empowering having a man at my feet. It makes me happy that they are enjoying themselves as I trample all over them and stick my heels down their throats, or right into their groins. OK, I have always probably been a bit of a pervert, but isn't everyone in some way or form?

Sitting against the wall, a towel under him, Boot Man would deliver his cock up to me, dangling it on the floor ready to be squashed under my boot and shouting, "Harder...harder," as I stamped on the limp sausage. He would love his body to be trampled underfoot, and especially having his nipples rubbed by the hard end of my heel. I suppose he was a mixture of Shoe Guy and Willy

Whacker—I'll tell you all about him later—with the exception that Boot Man liked to wank as I stuck a rubbered finger in his slack hole. Even a thumb sliding up his butt would make him quiver and come...not such a peculiar request as it turns out. Many a time I have been asked to shove a finger or two or even a butt plug up a straight man's bottom, just as he's about to come.

My Shoe Guy would be on his knees when I went in, crawling towards my feet when I sat on the edge of the bed. He loved to suck on my heels. He would lie on his back as I lowered a heel into his mouth, sucking on it greedily, pulling my shoe off to smell the inside. I would peel down the nylon stocking on one leg so my toes wriggled free. Taking hold of my foot like an unwrapped sweet, he would suck my toes one at a time, sticking his tongue in between each one while merrily wanking away. Then, rubbing his penis under my toes, he would ejaculate straight on to the base of my foot, lifting it up to lick the come from my sole.

Ultimate control—and I loved it! I was reliving the thrill as I padded into the kitchen on a snack hunt. Carry and Sukey were there, talking about an annoying client and how to take control of the situation when a bloke got too big for his boots.

Carry looked up at me, pulled out a chair, patted the seat invitingly, and asked me with a smile if I wanted a biscuit. I sat as she turned to Sukey and said, "See," motioning towards me with her hand.

"See what?" I piped up as they looked at each other.

"Carry was just saying you could easily get most people to do what you wanted with directive body language, or something." Sukey picked up a biccie from the tin.

"And what was the 'see' about?" I raised an eyebrow at Carry.

"I said I could get the next person who walked in to sit in a seat of my choosing, and in you walked and sat where I said."

"But all you did was just pull out a chair and say sit." I frowned.

"Exactly—I pulled out a chair, patted it, and gave you a reason to sit. Simple." She grinned at Sukey like a big ginger cat.

"So, the same applies to other things—you can get people to do what you want without them even knowing you are controlling the situation?"

Carry munched as she contemplated this. "Well, no, not everyone, but body language can make people do most things—suggestion is a powerful thing." She sipped her coffee as the buzzer went. "No rest for the wicked." She got up, leaving a trail of Hobnob crumbs in her wake. I, on the other hand, was happy to sit and contemplate the body language of Mr. Venice—if I remembered correctly, it was telling me that our pending trip to Paris held a lot of promise...

Testing Times

I dragged myself out of bed the next day and went in for my blood tests. I took the whole day off and tried to use it as a reading opportunity, taking my book to occupy me until they called me in. It felt like for ever, but it was only twenty-two minutes. The nurses were really friendly, joking, "Back again?" I was full of panic and asking myself a million questions—top of the list was why the hell was I still doing this to myself? Oh yes—the money—that's it!

I took a deep breath and closed my eyes as the blood was drawn.

Thinking of the money wasn't helping like it normally did when I had to do something foul and work-related, and when I left the hospital, I decided to blow out my classes for the day and take to bed with my book. I had a good sleep and tried not to think about going back in two weeks for the test results. I put my head in the sand; I'd worry about it later. Not very adult, but it helped at the time. Back on that horse? You bet!

Back on Duty

The most stupid question of all time? "What's a nice girl like you doing in a place like this?" was always a good one...

I don't really think they were ever fully prepared for my answer. It went something like: I'm smart enough to know I can make more money here than in a normal job, and I get all the sex I need with no strings attached. That's what I'm doing here!

The most stupid statement of all time? "You're beautiful, do you know that?" That's probably why you picked me then! Jeez, can't you come up with anything more original than that? What usually followed was a long list of every possible body part that was deemed beautiful, usually ones that no other person would have noticed, let alone mentioned...apparently, I have beautiful backs of my knees. Who'd have thought it?

Biggest lie of all time? "I don't want to be like the others, I want to please you...tell me what you like." If I have heard that once...yes, I have heard it more than a hundred times. It's completely unoriginal and just plain annoying after a while. If I wanted to be pleasured, I could get some willing chap to do that for me in my own time, but I don't—and that's certainly not why we work here. Sod's Law if I say the truth: I want a quick hard fuck. No bastard believes me!

Sometimes guys just like to talk. Yes, they like me to jump on them, but they also like the connection of talking, the "getting to know you," so in this job you need to be a good listener. People like to offload all their stress, and the girls in particular look for shoulders to cry on. Sometimes you can help, sometimes not. That is where the lounge came in handy—it was a place for gossiping and de-stressing but also a place for confiding in those to whom you were close. I had a lot of my best chats with Carry and

Bella there, particularly when we were the only ones around. If you sat in there for long enough, you'd manage to say hi to just about everyone who worked in the house.

Today was no exception and, after the crowds had dispersed, it was just me and Bella.

"Heard you might be moving on?" I nodded to Bella as she sat down on the sofa next to me.

"Mmm, thinking of a change. Have a friend who has just opened a house of discipline up north and she's looking for a weekend Domme—would be good to just deal with my pets in a fully equipped place rather than making do."

"So you would only be disciplining gimps then?" I looked, puzzled, at her.

"No, not just that—humiliation and other fetishes." I handed her the book she was reaching for. "Why, you looking for a change too?" she said, raising her eyebrows at me.

I gave her a smirk. "Nah, still got to be a student for a bit, don't think I could do what you do."

"Mmm, bit of rubber and a riding crop and you could do very well." She flicked through her trashy novel and winked at me.

"Ha ha—Like I look remotely dominant." I scowled and then fluttered my eyelashes.

"Well, you do when you do that! Could start a whole new fetish for cute Dommes."

The Rendezvous

J met Mr. Venice at Heathrow that Friday around 7
a.m. I felt a bit tired, as I'd just driven for four
hours to get there, but seeing him neatly turned out with
his nice shoes on soon perked me up. Occasionally, guys
with money can look a little scruffy, but on the whole
they'll always have nice shoes. Me, materialistic? What
do you think? I'd put up with a fair few assholes that
week and it was time for a pamper-me moment. Here was
my ticket.

We checked in and boarded the short flight to Paris,
collected our bags at the other end, and got a cab to the
Lancaster Hotel off the Rue de Berri right near the Arc de
Triomphe. We had a perfect afternoon lunching in a cute
bistro and then wandering over to the Louvre, spending
the afternoon looking at half-artistic nudes from the seven-
teenth century. Tired but full of Parisian buzz, we headed
back to the hotel in a cab to change for dinner. He had
bought me white undies, which were laid out on the bed
waiting for me when I came out of the shower.

He had gone to take a shower himself, leaving me to dress for dinner and no doubt whatever else would be on the menu later that night. The restaurant was quite romantic and we then went for a stroll along the Seine before heading back. As soon as we were in the room I peeled off my dress in front of the long wardrobe mirrors and sat astride him, the delicate white lace of the undies now the only barrier between us. I'd been keen to remain slightly detached, but I had to admit, I was quite enjoying myself! We both slept well that night, and he had a great start to the day when I woke him up with a blow-job. It obviously worked a treat as, after breakfast, he took me shopping to all the designer stores—we had a real laugh, as he made me try on lots of outrageous things before buying me some great outfits and shoes to match. Amazing what a bit of early morning effort can earn you!

We took all the shopping back to the hotel in a cab. My feet were killing me and we were carrying so many bags people were having trouble getting past us on the pavement. After dumping them all, I decided to put on one of my new skirts for lunch. Good move, as it was all rather posh. It's not as if I hadn't been to posh restaurants before, I just hadn't expected the meal to take so long—it was three hours in the end with all the courses, but at least it killed some time and meant I was getting to see Paris, rather than just Paris through a bedroom window! That afternoon we went to the Sacré-Coeur and I had my portrait sketched by a street artist in the square. We strolled around hand in hand and it all felt very romantic to be in such a great place with a sweet guy who seemed to enjoy my company and didn't simply want to shag me senseless. In fact, there seemed a strange lack of action on his part—I began to worry I had lost my magic touch! I decided things needed spicing up, so we went to the Crazy Horse for the kinky show and had a great time. We spent the rest of the night and most of the early morning in bed as he jumped on me as soon as we entered our room. I guess all those naked girls had done the trick—mission accomplished!

But while Mr. Venice was very attentive and generous, I was looking forward to getting back to some variety. The next morning, after nearly oversleeping, there was no time for morning nookie. I did my best to look shocked and disappointed—gosh, had I really accidentally turned off the alarm in my sleep? We left hurriedly for the airport. It was a quiet flight, and I pretended to doze as he held my hand for the hour. I was looking forward to having my own space back. I'd had a lovely time, but this whole "romance" thing was wearing rather thin, and it dawned on me that I liked life without romantic complications. He got held up at passport control, so I sat and waited and we got our bags together. I kissed him goodbye at the taxi rank and he pressed a £50 note into my hand for "petrol." I would have got so much more at the house! I suppose after all those new clothes, I must have bankrupted him! Smiling broadly, I waved him off. Ah, well, £50 was better than nothing, especially given that I had a brand-new Parisian wardrobe. What the hell, I'd had fun. I found my car in the airport car park eventually and drove back home, chatting to Layla on my mobile. She was at home, as she'd done the Saturday shift with Sanita. She'd just woken up and was desperate to hear all the news while sipping her wake-up coffee—I don't know why, as I would only be forced to tell her all over again when I got back to the flat. Predictably, when I arrived back I was greeted by two overexcited flatmates dancing around the lounge as soon as I opened my case, trying on my new shoes and flouncing around in my designer gear. I phoned Mr. Venice later in the day to say thanks for such a lovely time and for all the gifts, as by now I had found £500 he'd tucked inside one of the new handbags. What is it they say about silver linings?

Tuesday 23rd June

All-day shift 10:30 a.m.–1 a.m.
2 x Gemini, one with Ricky (The Manager), one with Layla = £30
14 x normal service + tips = £290
Minus £20 receptionist's fee
Total earned: £300

The Manager was a young guy in his late thirties, although he looked much younger, with short dark hair and boyish looks. I discovered just how funny he was on his first visit when I did a Gemini on him with Ricky. Armed with a strawberry yoghurt and no spoon, he proceeded to spread it over us and lick it off! You have to admire a creative mind that can use strawberry yoghurt as a sex aid! He is one guy I doubt I will ever forget. In a good way, though.

It was one of the messiest sessions I have had, and the three of us were in hysterics. We must have looked a sight going back into the girls' lounge, hair and make-up all over the place, covered in yoghurt. He came in on my next shift, and from then on I became his favourite. There would be a brief five-minute interlude on the bed and the rest of the time we would lie back, tickle, and chat until time was up. He cheered me up no end.

Results Day

J ambled down to the clinic the next afternoon, as they wouldn't give me the results over the phone. I walked in and was ushered straight into a small room. "Negative" was all I heard, along with lots of rustling paper as leaflets were thrust in my direction telling me how to take care of my sexual health—as if I didn't know already. That's the thing with these work-related accidents—people just assume you are careless, when it couldn't be further from the truth.

On my way out, the nurse shouted, "See you Sunday." It turned out she was popping round to the house to give us a slideshow. The mind boggled, but all I was interested in was the fact that I was clear and could get on with life. The ladies from the local GUM clinic came to the house once every six months to answer any questions we had. Even girls not working that shift came in to see them. I knew two of the ladies; the third was not familiar, but she was a psychiatrist for the clinic and very curious about what we all did. If I hadn't known she was from the clinic, I'd have thought, given her excessive nosiness, that she was a reporter, and that would've freaked me out.

It's not that we hated the media full stop, it's just that it is all about exposing people, and lives could be ruined if people found out what we did, and they made things so much worse with their salacious portrayal of houses like ours. That kind of negative exposure can do real harm— Sukey was here to prove it. Now that she was back from hospital we heard the full story. Her hubby had known she was supplementing their income by working on the game—but he didn't mind until one of his friends found out. God knows how. He promptly told everyone, and Sukey's husband denied knowing anything about it. He then took his embarrassment out on Sukey and she ended up having a small stroke and a broken jaw from the repeated blows. She was still recovering, but she wasn't the same girl—the sparkle had gone. Her daughters had been put into care while she was in hospital and she'd been allowed to have them back only when she agreed to leave and have a restraining order put on her loony hubby. The whole situation was because of gossip. If it had been in the papers, she said, he probably would have killed her and their girls would have been motherless.

The scary feeling of who knows what and the worry that they are going to use the knowledge against you is the hardest thing about this kind of work. The misconceptions, the shame, being judged because of what you do. The image of the filthy, diseased whore always makes me laugh, as we are technically one of the sexually safest demographic groups in the country.

For a start, these visits from nurses did raise our awareness. We would watch the slideshow, taking it all in. The big screen would show graphic pictures of genitals both with and without sexually transmitted infections, so we knew what to look for. God, all those diseased privates nearly put me off sex altogether!

You have to really love sex—or the money—not to let pictures like that freak you out. That kind of seminar would be the best sex education you could offer to teenagers; it would probably have put me off sex for good...well, maybe not, but at least I would have known the pitfalls! You hear so much crap, and films like *Pretty Woman* have a lot to bloody answer for. People really believe that rubbish. "Why can't I kiss you? Is it because you don't really like me?" No, you idiot, I don't kiss you for hygiene reasons! You can catch stuff from kissing. Can you imagine? The bugs spread throughout the house were bad enough with us cooped up all day together—it only took the girl with the weakest immune system to get the sniffles and all hell broke loose with the rota—imagine what it would be like if I was kissing every bloke who came in? A smile might not be the only thing I was left with! On a typical day when business was good, we had anything from fifty to over a hundred clients through our doors. If everyone kept on getting colds it would just keep the clients away and, at the end of the day, as good as the sex can be, we were in it for the money too.

Kissing is one thing, but don't get me started on OWO. Fair enough if everyday folks indulge *sans* rubber and don't share my obsession with the condom. It's not up to me to educate the public, but I know people who have lived to regret not taking precautions. I had a friend, not in the sex industry, who caught oral herpes and it worked its way down her throat and into her lungs before she realized what was going on. This was from a new "boyfriend" she had just met. Poor thing wasn't very experienced and just believed him when he said she couldn't catch anything as he begged her to give him Oral Without a condom. They split up when she started to get ill. The irony was that he got treated and she died a slow, painful death in a hospital bed. Ladies, you're smart people: get a clue! Men will try anything ("You can't get anything from sucking it without a rubber"..."I'm clean"..."Just suck it once, I promise I won't come in your mouth"..."I can't get it up with a rubber on"...) Ha, men. Love 'em, but those who think like that get no respect from any girl, especially not a working one. When I hear those pleas now, all I can see in my head is that screen with all those grim reminders of what the consequences can be if you don't protect yourself ...Ignorant men aren't so sexy. I have one deal-breaker—no rubber, no bounce! If a guy had problems wearing a rubber, he would wank without one. That suited me fine, as I loved to watch him shoot his load all over my nipples, giving me a tickly feeling across my chest, the little pink points glistening in the sticky warmness. It's so dirty.

Summertime
and Bad Times

*T*he summer arrived and I began to feel desperate for some kind of escape, for a return to life before the house, when everything was free and easy and I could be myself. I guess, in reality, I didn't really have a clue who I was any more, I'd forgotten how to be "normal." It had been nearly a year since I'd started working at the house, and although I couldn't complain—I was well looked after, had lots of regs, very few assholes on the books, and the money was great—I started to crave something else. Control.

In a bid to get some time out, I started to drive down to the coast on my days off. Layla and Sanita would sometimes come with me if they had the day off too, and we would spend time on the beach, reading, revising, and sketching, just being ourselves. I had the money to go where I wanted and do what I liked. It was a golden summer until...

Carlos, the drug-dealing stalker: I didn't know what a problem he was going to be when I met him; he seemed a nice guy—quiet, polite, and well-respected by all. I was pretty interested in him, he was gorgeous and one of Layla's group of friends, none of whom knew what we did for a living, so he came with a good recommendation. Carlos seemed pretty interested in me and I hoped it would come to something. I hate the whole "dating" situation where you have to declare your intentions—despite what I do for a living, I am quite an old-fashioned kinda girl in the real world! I got my wish when he invited me out to dinner—I was delighted and felt reassured, as I knew that Layla's prick radar was very finely tuned. With that in mind, I happily went to a local restaurant with him a few days later. I didn't tell Layla about the date as I hadn't seen her for a few days—she was working bloody hard saving up for the holiday somewhere hot she had promised herself. But I didn't need her permission: Carlos was cute and I thought it was about time I had some action in my private life—I had been living like a nun out of office hours!

He picked me up in a *very* expensive car, which I thought was a bit strange, as it didn't suit his casual pub image. As the conversation kicked off it became clear that he didn't have a job and he avoided discussing the issue, which obviously made me more intrigued. Being a student, I didn't need a job, so no first-date revelations from me! Despite having a nice time there was still a niggling feeling that something was wrong. I don't usually ignore my instincts, but everyone seemed to like him and he was real eye-candy, so I kissed him goodbye and arranged another date. Things progressed well and I was enjoying being romanced—after months of work-related sex, it felt good to be wooed. Mr. Venice must have been the wrong kind of man for me, because I was definitely enjoying this courtship. I began to think I might be starting to fall for him—and then I found out what he did for a living. Drugs are something I can't deal with. Even when I like the person involved, I just don't want anything to do with that set-up. I don't hate people who do drugs, I just hate what they do to people, and although Carlos didn't do drugs himself, I really didn't want any part of it. In my line of work, it was asking for trouble from the law should anything kick off.

The bottom line was that he just wasn't as cool as I'd thought. He was starting to get very clingy, turning up on my doorstep at all hours, phoning me and demanding to know where I was all the time, which really didn't suit my chosen profession and the antisocial hours I kept.

The final straw came when he broke in. He didn't take anything, just rearranged our furniture, and I had no idea why. I knew it had to be him, as his goons had been hanging around outside most nights; I'd noticed them sitting in a parked car across the street and sniggering when I arrived home. Layla wasn't happy either and had words with him, but he said that if she had a problem she should find another dealer. I had no idea she bought pot from him—no wonder they were so friendly!

I reported him straight away for harassment, but the police said they couldn't really do anything unless he threatened me. Obviously, I didn't mention he was a dealer, or what I did to pay the bills. They advised me ("not officially, you understand") to change my name and move on.

Fat lot of help that was. I was powerless and Carlos knew it. Day and night his idiot mates would sit in a car opposite the flat watching me come and go. Although nothing really happened, I felt under siege and things didn't feel the same. I was utterly paranoid (with reason), I knew it was only a matter of time before Carlos and his cronies followed me to work and my secret was out. I began to have nightmares. One of the most bizarre was that he would be the punter sitting in reception as I said my hello, or that I would walk into a room about to start a shift and he would be face down on the bed as I began my massage...What made it worse was that things were definitely strange in the house, too: I couldn't put my finger on it, but paranoia had started to hit the girls. We were all starting to think we were being watched or filmed in the rooms, and it really felt like it might be time to leave. Rumours were rife—one of the girls said that if you entered a members' pay site on the internet you could see secret-camera footage of the Ballroom. It sounded a little far-fetched, and it turned out that the girl in question was always late and was being watched by Mrs. B, so she had a motive for spreading rumours. Still, it gave me an uneasy feeling, and I began to scan the rooms for spycams before and after each session.

As the summer wore on I wasn't comfortable either at home or work. This feeling was compounded by the fact that our cosy little flat, our haven, had been invaded yet again. We'd all gone out to do the weekly food shop together; it had become a communal activity ever since I bought my car. Layla had run out of cigarettes and, as neither Sanita nor I smoked, we couldn't offer any, so we set off earlier than usual to build in the cigarette run. We stopped for a coffee on the way back and decided to see a film. Returning later that afternoon, we unloaded our shopping and packed it away in the tiny kitchen. It was Layla who noticed the cigarette ash in the bath as she went for a pee. How had that got there? We'd all had showers that morning, and the bath had been spotless when we left. The ash certainly didn't belong to Layla, as she smoked only in her room and, anyway, she hadn't had any cigarettes left.

We phoned the rental agency and they confirmed that the landlord had been in the flat that morning with a plumber. Apparently, it had been an emergency, as they thought our washing machine was leaking through to the flat underneath. There were obvious problems with this theory. Firstly, the machine hadn't even been on and, secondly, we'd have noticed if it had been leaking that morning as we had done two washloads before we left. Thirdly, we all had mobile phones, and the agent had our numbers to call if he needed access to the flat. The fact was, no one had phoned to say they were coming round, meaning they had entered the flat without our consent. What was more, I wasn't sure if our stuff had been disturbed—my bedroom door was open but I was sure I had closed it before I'd left that morning.

I went straight out and bought a locked box in which to keep my money and important details, including my work diary. The whole thing felt utterly creepy—for all we knew, whoever had been in the flat had been rifling through our undies looking for a pair to sniff or something. Being paranoid was the norm in the house as we dealt with weirdos every day, but this was wrong, this was supposed to be our home. It didn't help that we all kept such abnormal hours and the flat was empty a lot of the time. We started to worry that the landlord, or anyone he'd given keys to, could walk in on us at any moment. I'd already changed the locks after Carlos broke in; now we changed them for a second time and decided not to hand the keys out to anyone, not even the landlord. But it looked like the invasion had just begun and my fighting spirit was starting to fade.

Being under pressure at the flat was one thing, but gradually work began to lose its gloss, too—business was slowing down even more and girls were moving on. Then Suzie got caught out and gave us all pause for thought. We were a sensible bunch in the house—no amount of money could persuade us to take risks with our sexual health, despite the fact that sometimes the money offered was impressive. But unfortunately for Suzie, she liked to push the boundaries, and she quite often did extras, especially blow-jobs without a rubber...until it all went very wrong with one particular rough reg.

I had been enjoying a few days off from the house, doing chores, finishing off some coursework, and generally catching up with myself, when Layla came crashing through the front door looking distracted and threw herself down on the sofa.

"What's up?" I asked. "Bad day at the office?"

"You could say that. You know the new big prick who has been coming in and hassling Suzie?"

"Yeah, quite cute? The one who calls her his own personal little porn star?"

"That's the one. Well, he has been droning on about her sucking him off without a rubber, and this time he offered her a huge wad of cash to have full, unprotected sex as well—obviously desperate. Anyway, she tried to laugh it off and explained the rules for the umpteenth time, and he just flipped. He slapped her on to the bed, pinned her down by her neck, and before she knew what was happening, he was inside her without a condom. It was all over in a flash, and he had already come. She hit the alarm, Mr. B came charging in and nearly beat the guy to a pulp. Upsetting thing was that he got away before Mr. B could finish off the job, ran off so quickly he even left his shoes behind."

I was horrified for her. "What a nightmare, how is Suzie taking it?"

"Quite calmly really, there weren't any hysterics. She just looked in shock, to be honest. Mrs. B took her up to the flat with an ice pack on her face."

"Jeez, poor girl. I hope she's OK."

"She'll be fine, she's a tough girl, that one."

The irony was that we had been chatting over tea and biscuits first thing that morning about how slow business had been and what we were going to do. Suzie had mentioned stripping—she reckons it's great money and all you have to do is get your clothes off: no actual action required! After this, I expect she'll be the next one to move on. Frankly, who could blame her?

As I shut the curtains tightly against the lurking presence sitting in the car outside, I was having the same feeling myself.

Sunday 19th July

All-day shift 10:30 a.m.–1 a.m.
1 Gemini with Layla (Alan, the old arrogant bastard) = £15
13 x normal service (including Mr. Make-up; Chinese Jinnie—
£5 tip and 3 regulars: Brian, Jeff, and Ray) = £265
Minus £20 receptionist's fee
Total earned: £260

*M*r. Make-up wanted me to be a stereotypical whore. He brought in tight, transparent clothing he had bought from charity shops; it all smelled a bit mothbally. He handed it all over to the receptionist for the lucky chosen one to wear. Cheap ankle chains over stockings was his favourite look and he insisted that I wear heavy make-up, which he wanted me to put on in full view, too, topped off with bright-red lipstick plastered on like I was a clown. He would be in raptures when I told him I'd had loads of clients that day and that I was feeling particularly sore and swollen.

"You're a dirty slut," was the enthusiastic reply as he bent me over, pulling up the tight skirt I was wearing, exposing my knickerless bum. He proceeded to pump away, calling me all sorts of names—nothing very original, really. At that point, I'd been working there long enough for those types of remarks not to have any impact whatsoever.

Banging away till I was well and truly past feeling sore and on the way to being completely numb, he seemed to take huge pride in this epic farce. It wasn't unusual—the occasional client would think his prowess depended on his staying power, no matter how tedious it was for me. I mentally ticked off my weekly chore list in my head. I could probably have used my lipstick on the mirror by the side of the bed to remind me exactly what I needed to do and he wouldn't even have noticed. It might have been pushing my luck to ask him his opinion in mid-flow, though: "Mmm, mm, yess!...harder harder...What do you think I should buy my dad for his birthday? You're a bloke...do you think he would like a laser-level tape measure or maybe a camera? He's been dropping hints for both...but I'm just not sure."

Maybe I could hustle him along if I squeezed a bit more? I should have paid more attention to those pelvic-floor exercises the girls had been practising in the lounge the previous week while watching *Oprah*. The floor had been full of girls thrusting their hips off the ground, a weird sight and in complete contrast with the normal lounging around that went on in there.

I suddenly came to and gazed around the room. Was he still going? Yep, the bed was still moving a bit. It's truly amazing, the things that run through your head when you're really bored. I decided I'd better get some shopping in tomorrow afternoon and I mentally sifted through the bathroom cupboards at home...definitely running out of Tampax...and bleach...more lube, better check the washing powder, too. My roaming eyes rested on the decor—that picture wasn't right in here and the frame was the wrong colour and dusty, especially from this angle. It needed a really good clean.

"Mmmm. YES!" I shouted, trying to urge him on and get it over and done with. What did he want—a gold bloody medal?

I dunked my biscuit in my lukewarm tea. The kitchen was quiet. Where was everyone? The bell hadn't buzzed in a while—and if it did, it looked like I'd be doing the hello on my own! Cebell was on reception flicking through a copy of a fashion magazine, although it would take more than one backdated mag to put her right. Given she was the first thing people saw as they entered the house, I couldn't quite see how she got away with looking like she did, but Mrs. B seemed oblivious.

I was engrossed in my latest book when Suzie popped her head round the door. "Hey, babe, how you doing? Layla told me about that bastard the other week. You OK? You're back to work quickly—what did the nurse say?"

"Thanks, hon, you know the score—too soon to test for anything yet, just have to wait now. The worst bit.

Actually, it's a real headfuck, but I can't stand hysterics—no use crying over spilt milk and all that. Anyway, I can't afford to mope around—I need the cash." She put the kettle on and searched around for something to eat.

Denial, I thought. She was obviously adopting the head-in-the-sand approach, and who could blame her?

"God, it's like a morgue in here—where is everyone?" Suzie gestured wildly, swinging the half-full kettle.

"I don't really know what is going on—I've never known it so quiet. There hasn't been much business for a while. If it wasn't for my regs, I don't know where I'd be."

"Well, between you and me, I'm thinking of cutting my ties and heading to London. If anything, that prick did me a favour and forced me to make my mind up. I've been dithering for ages, but it's time to move on. I just don't feel safe, and there's a weird vibe in the house, it's like all the fun has gone. There's something going on, I can feel it. Thought I might try some stripping. Being realistic, I might have caught something, and I need a back-up plan. It's risk-free money." We sat at the table together, both lost in thought. Suzie broke the silence. "What about you? What's your plan?"

"Uni course is nearly up. Unfortunately, the same can't be said for Carlos. He's still hanging around like a bad smell. Don't know really, I'm still giving it some thought," I pondered.

"Well, I'd quit while I was ahead if I were you. Go out on top, no pun intended!"

Maybe she had a point.

Making Plans

When Layla came home, I relayed the conversation I'd had with Suzie about London and stripping. Layla was always up for anything and urged me to consider it. So that's how I found myself driving to London, taking Suzie to a strip gig in a small, dingy basement pub. Shortly after our chat, Suzie had found out she had gonorrhea. She quit the house immediately and so far, she hadn't had a flip-out. I guess she was keeping busy as a distraction, plus she hadn't stopped going on about how much money could be earned in London stripping, and I wanted to see if it was true.

Layla was fascinated, stating that, if Suzie "with the state her body was in" could earn a packet, then we would have no worries coining it in. What the hell, we say hello to drunks in our underwear on a Saturday night, so how hard could stripping be? Suzie's strip gig was a private affair run by some guy she hadn't even met. Layla and I thought it sounded a bit too much like a jack-off gig, but Suzie was convinced it was "just stripping," as the guy had promised!

I was interested in what it was like to strip and I was beginning to feel as if working at the house was more hassle than it was worth, especially with all that was going on. I was also getting a bit bored of it all. Suzie didn't mind us coming to check her gig out, as it was safer to have people with her. Plus, although she had quit the house, she still wanted to keep in touch with those of us who were still there.

We arrived at the club and made our way down to the bar. We were greeted by a room full of men. Two women dressed in short skirts were standing next to the bar with a tall man with a dodgy moustache. Suzie went to greet him, and then headed straight off to the toilet to change.

Layla and I managed to squeeze into a corner of the room. We ordered a drink and tried to fade into the background. "If anyone touches me, I am so leaving. Sod Suzie," Layla whispered in my ear. "Me too," I squeaked back, sinking into the wall with my...well, I think it was supposed to be orange juice...

The host welcomed everyone using a mike rigged up to a small sound system in the corner and, putting on some music, introduced the first woman. She began to strip, moving around the room with a metal tin for tips, sitting on guys' laps and grinding away. Stripping off and shoving her breasts in the guys' faces, having made her way around the room, she was naked by the time she got to a mat in the middle of the floor. Producing a vibrator from her huge bag, she got down on all fours and started writhing and masturbating till she came and came again. Although not the best viewing I've ever had, quite frankly I'd seen much worse, so I certainly wasn't as shocked as some people in the room seemed to be.

Picking up her stuff, she left to a round of applause. Now it was Suzie's turn. She moved around the room with a collecting glass, stripping out of her flimsy gear and covering her chest in squirty cream, her nipples in marshmallows, getting guys to have a nibble. Finishing her set, she strode off to the bathroom—she wasn't too happy after the last guy had tried to shove his finger up her ass as she sat on his lap.

The next woman was already doing the rounds with a collecting glass. She was an unattractive blonde who looked just like a dowdy housewife. She'd gone round with her container during Suzie's finale, even shaking it at us at one point, till I pointed out that Suzie was still doing her set across the room and any tips to be collected were hers. She shrugged and continued.

The housewife blonde did much the same as the first lady but ended by fisting herself and sucking off a random bloke without a rubber. She was joined by the first girl, who was naked again. They then proceeded to do some girl-on-girl 69 action and finished by offering to relieve some of the guys who were pleasuring themselves while watching the spectacle. They were pretty much mobbed, and Suzie stepped in to help. Layla and I sat there, a bit stunned—not by the scene itself, but by the fact that the two girls had done oral without protection.

This was another world, very far away from the one we were used to, and I didn't like it one bit. Layla and I declined offers to join the orgy-like mess in front of us. It started to break up, as most of the wanking men had finished anyway. Suzie, covered in the sticky end result, managed to disentangle herself from giving hand jobs—

luckily she'd managed to get away without having to suck anyone off and went to the loos to wash down.

In a huddled twosome, we drained our drinks and started to feel a little uneasy in the stuffy room, which now smelt of musty sex. As soon as Suzie joined us again we were on our way. She waved an enthusiastic goodbye to the moustached host behind the bar, grabbing her bag tightly. We rushed up the stairs and back to the relative safety of my car.

"God! Lying bastard! He wouldn't give me the £50 he promised till I joined in at the end," she puffed.

"You only got fifty quid?" demanded an outraged Layla.

"Well, and tips—not bad for not having sex," Suzie said, grinning, shaking the tin as she got in the car and emptied her can of coins out on her lap.

Layla and I just looked at each other. It was priceless. It dawned on us that we hadn't realized one simple thing: what Suzie considered raking it in didn't mean remotely the same thing to us. It was late by the time we dropped her off. London had been a five-hour drive there and five hours back, and I was shattered—both by the drive and by what I had seen. I don't know how much Suzie made in the end, but it couldn't have been much. She hadn't expected that level of involvement with the crowd—she and her agent had been led to believe it really was a simple striptease gig—it really was more than just stripping.

At last, Layla and I arrived home. It was really late and we found that the landlord had been in the flat. He hadn't been able to reach the agent as it was the weekend, and he didn't like the fact that he didn't have a key, so he had had the new lock drilled out and replaced. Christ! That meant we were locked out until we could get hold of the agent on Monday morning. We went to the sauna a few hours before it was due to close and Mrs. B offered to put us up in her spare bedroom above the lounge on the top floor. We weren't really allowed upstairs, as it was the bosses' flat, out of bounds, and the only door leading upstairs was normally locked, so this was a real honour.

Before we went to bed, we sat in the girls' lounge with a mug of hot chocolate each, complaining to the others about our bastard landlord.

"I am sort of having the same problem with mine at the moment," commiserated Bella, sprawled out on one of the sofas nearby. "Thinking of moving on," she sighed and winked at me.

"Maybe it's time for us, too?" Layla said to me. She had a point: the situation with Carlos had really been grinding me down, and now our home was being invaded. Maybe I was being paranoid, but were the two connected? To make matters worse, I didn't know it at the time, but that was going to be the last I saw or heard from Bella. She just disappeared in a poof of Domme dust. She was such a fixture in the house, I just didn't think she would ever leave, even though she had mentioned the house of discipline up north. We missed her terribly, and it proved to be the catalyst I needed to think about a life away from the house.

I got up early the next morning. Layla was already up; I could hear her putting the coffee machine on in Mr. and Mrs. B's kitchen. I started looking for the bathroom, still half asleep. I turned right in the dimly lit corridor, only to be confronted by a washing machine blocking the way. There was a dark staircase that wound down round a corner behind the offending item, but you could only see the stairs if you were right in front of the machine. I realized that they probably led downstairs, either into or next to one of our working rooms. I grabbed Layla in the kitchen as she rubbed her eyes, still half asleep herself.

"Shhh," I motioned, and pulled her with me, dragging her arm. I pointed over to the stairs behind the washing machine and said, "You've been here longer than me—where does it go?"

"Shit, I have no idea! I thought we only used the one door to get in here. I know we have the back door, but that is strictly for clients, so they don't have to see anyone when they leave, especially not the bosses." She was wide-eyed by now. We peered over the machine.

"Do you think that's how Mr. B gets back in and how he escaped when we were raided?" I said.

Mr. B would disappear on a Sunday to go out and get a paper, using the front door. You could see him on the cameras. He would then reappear some hours later in the lounge, despite the fact that we hadn't seen him come back in on the cameras. We always assumed it was because Sunday mornings were quite busy and we had just missed him coming back.

"Could be," Layla whispered, pushing me back towards the machine. "Go and have a look—I'll keep guard."

I have no idea what we would have done if the bosses had come out of their room, which was just down the hall. Luckily, they had been up late with a drunken punter, so it was probably still too early for them. I climbed over the big white box in my bare feet, T-shirt, and thong, secretly pleased to be the one on the mission.

I crept down a few steps and peered left around the bend. My eyes were getting accustomed to the dark, and I could see a few more steps and then it levelled out, straight into a landing heading towards the back of the house.

"It goes along to the back," I whispered to Layla, poking my head back around the corner. "Shhh, shhh," she said and flicked her hand at me to go further.

I edged forward and noticed a blacked-out window on the landing to my right. That was just plain weird, as it wasn't like the windows you normally see on internal walls. I pushed it open a bit, as far as it would go. Looking in, all I could see in the dark was a smooth board in front, but if I looked either side I could see a strip of light and some dark wallpaper.

I closed the window and continued along the corridor, then down some steps and ended up at a door with peeling paint and a heavy lock on it. I padded quickly up the bare concrete steps and clambered back over the washing machine, reaching for Layla's hand as I went.

"It goes outside," I said in her ear, my heart racing. She nodded, and we crept to the kitchen, out of earshot.

"Mystery solved," Layla smiled, reaching for the coffee pot.

"Well, yes, but there was something else," I murmured.

"What?" She turned and faced me, looking far more content now she had her shot of caffeine.

"There was an internal window that I think must look into one of the rooms. You know that mirror in the Mirror Room? The one that's above the bed, a few inches down from the ceiling? I think the window is behind that." She didn't look too bothered.

"So maybe the mirror is just blocking the window so the clients don't freak out."

"You mean like the one that covers that old door downstairs in the Parlour, which is actually bricked up?" A full-length mirror had been put there to hide the door, as the clients were afraid someone would walk in or peek through the big keyhole.

"Yeah, like that. Could you see through the mirror? Was it a one-way one?" Layla queried.

That had been running through my mind, too, but it was so dark on both sides I couldn't be certain.

"Not sure, but anyone standing behind it could hear what was going on in that room." She looked at me and nodded again as I said that.

"Right, we'll have to be careful what we say in the Mirror Room then, in the future. I think we should keep quiet about it, otherwise Mrs. B will know we have been snooping."

Maybe the spying rumours were true after all; maybe Mrs. B didn't only rely on the house snitch. She did seem to know our every thought and movement.

"Well, now we really know why they put the new girls in that room, and it's not because it's closer to the lounge so they don't get lost. Clever but very sneaky...better tell Sanita, and drop the subject before we are overheard."

There was a lot to mull over. I wasn't too bothered if Mr. B got his kicks perving, but left us alone—fair enough—but I wondered if Mrs. B spied on us too? The paranoia was completely taking over. I had been thinking the walls had ears for a long time, but I wasn't indignant now; in fact, in a strange way, it was nice to know I wasn't cracking up. But things were changing, and it was a shock to find that I wasn't as safe as I had thought I was—I didn't like that aspect of it one bit.

And Now We Come
to the End...

$\mathcal{I}$t was getting chilly, and the end of summer was in sight. Work was very slow, but at least we now knew that it was down to the fact that we had a competing house and, typically, our customers were trying out the new girls. People were still on holiday, I was doing OK, but the lull was really rousing unrest in the other girls. Plus, in spite of my usual rational self, I couldn't get that mirror out of my mind. Suzie was playing on my mind—London had been so good for her, allowing for the fresh start she so desperately needed, and the money she was now earning stripping sounded great. Clearly that first club had been a complete dive. The idea started to grow on me and, in the end, I thought, why the hell not? It couldn't all be as bad as her strip gig last time, not in the proper places surely? And, anyway, my course was now finished and I really had to think about the future.

Carlos and his idiotic mates were still following me around now and again, proving that they weren't the types just to let things drop. Me, Layla, and Sanita discussed London again, and I decided to drive up for the weekend to see if we could get work. A group of us went—Layla, Helen—who'd recently joined the house—and Helen's twenty-year-old daughter, Haley. Helen was very open about what she did for a living, and although Haley had no problem with it, she was too scared to work in a house like her mum, so stripping seemed perfect.

We arrived in London and booked two rooms in a sprawling hotel. Driving around that morning, we found adverts for regular hostess and dancing girls in the back of a London paper and Helen called up straight away and got us an audition in the West End. After cleaning up and depositing our bags in our rooms, we made our way to the interview. We didn't have to bring anything with us, it was just a chat (and an opportunity for them to give us the once-over).

We were met at the door of the nightclub by a young blonde woman in a suit. It took a while for our eyes to get used to the darkness inside, but soon we could see that it was an impressive place. It had a big stage with the obligatory poles, a swanky-looking bar, and, above all, it looked clean.

The woman ushered us inside, chatting away as she shuffled us down a corridor. We finally arrived outside an office and, after answering all the questions we threw at her, she asked us to strip privately in her office. We didn't have to do a dance of any sort—it was just so she could see if our bodies were suitable: no tattoos, scars, etc. After all that, only I got offered a job! Getting out her camera to take a

Polaroid of my face for door ID, she said I could start that night if I turned up at eight. I was told to bring a dress, that was it.

I really didn't want to do it on my own, but the girls talked me into it. The manageress had turned down Layla because she was a little too overweight, Helen because she was too old, and Haley because she was too tall and gangly, plus, the few tattoos she had didn't suit the image at the club. Tact was obviously a requisite of her job as the girls didn't feel offended. I felt uneasy but the girls were excited for me and were going out on the town to celebrate while I did my first shift.

I arrived at the door before eight, carrying my backpack with everything I thought I might need, and was shown to a small dark room to change with a few other girls. Most of them were new too. I found out that the more experienced girls, the ones who worked for agents, got the nice dressing room around the corner; we, on the other hand, were stuck in this room without a mirror. The people weren't overly friendly, and it soon became clear there was a big social divide among the girls. There were the ones who were just dancers, and then there were the ones who would meet men outside the club and exchange sex for money, which wasn't allowed. I kept my mouth shut. One of the girls was quite vocal in her disapproval and seemed to hate the rest with a vengeance for making her job seem disreputable, but as I was new I decided to keep my head down and avoid the politics.

It soon became apparent that the more popular girls were the ones with the bigger boobs; either that, or I was starting to get tit envy. It was a bit of both, I think. The stripping was incredibly boring, especially compared to what I usually got up to at the sauna. At the end of the shift when I was leaving, two of the girls walked me to my car, which was nice of them. One of them announced she was going to have a boob job the following week. They both claimed it was a great investment, as you automatically earned more, and that I should consider it. Great, just the boost I needed at the end of a long night: two girls I didn't know saying I should have a boob job.

Well, the grand total at the end of the night said it all really. I earned £50. I got to keep all of it because it was my first day, but I hated every moment of it. What's the point in teasing men? Taking their money and then not being able to have my wicked way with them? I went back to the hotel room to shower and scrub myself. I felt dirty and cheap, and my mind was buzzing. I didn't know how the girls on stage did it...hats off to them...or should that be pants off? Definitely not my kind of thing, and there was so much bitching. Maybe it was just that club? Maybe a bit more of an upmarket one would be better? Whatever the set-up elsewhere, I decided stripping would be deeply frustrating.

I had hoped to earn enough to cover my personal goal, from what I should have earned in the house at that time during my absence that weekend shift. Also to cover a cab back to the hotel and make a bigger profit too would have been nice, but no such luck. I returned the following night to see if it would be any better, but it wasn't. I earned £80, good for a new girl, so I am told, but the house took £40 and my parking cost £20, so I felt even worse.

But it was decision time—should I stay at the house and work full-time now my course was finished and hope the situation improved and that my regs kept me ticking over until business picked up again, or should I take this way out and a chance to move to London for more adventure?

I opted for London and a fresh start and called up the manageress to say I'd take the job but I needed to sort out somewhere to stay in London first. She gave me the phone number of one of her dancers, Claudia, as she had a room to let in Holborn, fairly near the club.

I arranged to go and meet Claudia one afternoon in London so I could see the flat. She seemed a bit aloof, but her English was quite bad so it was hard to judge. The flat was in a red-bricked council block close to Oxford Street, small and bare, but OK. My proposed room was poky, with a mattress on the floor and not much else, but I could move in two weeks' time.

Claudia was a tall, skinny, brunette ex-model (or so she said) from Russia, with a real attitude. She was here to learn English and was "just dancing" at the club (I was snootily informed) to pay her way, but I got the impression there was a sugar daddy floating around in the background. The flat was immaculate, although there wasn't any stuff around to make it untidy. The windows in the lounge didn't even have curtains, and a bare lightbulb hung from every ceiling, but that could all be fixed. I shook her bony hand and said I would take it. It felt like the right thing to do for the short term, even though the weekly rent was more than I paid per month with Layla and Sanita.

I went back to start packing, and I wasn't the only one—Layla and Sanita had decided to up sticks too. They could have easily got another girl to move in, as it was a nice flat, but I think they just wanted a clean slate too. The landlord was still acting strangely, finding excuses to come round. It had all got out of hand, and we were feeling vulnerable. I don't blame them one bit for wanting to move. Plus, business at the sauna had almost ground to a halt.

Layla and Sanita started flat-hunting in earnest. It became a hobby, with local papers covered in red rings scattered around the flat. It would have been so much easier if Layla had finished her course at the same time as me, as she wanted to go to London too, but she had another year to go and Sanita had no idea what she wanted to do. So it was going to be me on my tod then. I was not going to include the sulky Claudia in the friendship equation yet. I'd deal with her later. The main aim was just to get out and start afresh. There was no reason to stay in a town with no prospects—it was time to relocate and continue my life studies!

Friday 28th August: The Final Shift

Morning shift 10:30 a.m.–6 p.m. (sick cover)

6 x normal service + tips (including Al the Wood Joiner—big!; Shoe Guy; Jimmy, who comes in after the factory closes; Jeff the regular; Alan the Chemical Engineer and Mr. Willy Whacker) = £140

No receptionist's fee

Total earned: £140

Clients in total: 723

Willy Whacker had a long, skinny willy that didn't ever get properly hard, even after a body-to-body rubdown and a long sucking. There wasn't much of an erection for me to sit on so, kneeling at the side of the bed, he would watch me masturbate. My legs swinging off the bed, he would sneak his head between them, taking short sniffs like an interested dog, and would then resort to licking my stocking-clad thigh and, with one hand, whack his deflated willy up and down with long, hard slaps upon his lap.

Sometimes he would hit it against any other available hard object. I had to try so hard not to laugh. All this went on until, still soft, he would tug at it, twisting his balls at the same time with his free hand. Then he would come all the way up his chest, with me trying to catch the mess with tissues so he didn't stain the carpet. Nice chap, but what good is a thirteen-inch-cock if you can't use it? Not that I like them long—quite the opposite, in fact, especially if a long one is coming at me from behind. It can be damn painful and usually makes me want to pee. What a way to close the door on an extraordinary year—possibly the best client of them all.

Signing Off

In the end, I called Mrs. B, saying I was moving on and to cancel the rest of my shifts. I couldn't face the whole goodbye fuss from everyone, so I thought it was best just to leave. She was upset but wished me the best and said that I knew where they were if I wanted to come back. So that was that. I think she had been expecting it really.

I had kept a logbook throughout the year. No matter how tired I was, I always wrote down the details of each shift, how many clients, any regulars' tips, evening or all-day shift—anything I could remember really. It looks like a lot to some, but when you consider you are risking your life for £20 a shot, it most certainly isn't megabucks—the lies and the sacrifice to your health, not to mention the lack of social life, far outweigh the positives, like regular sex and lots of cash.

I was lucky, dead lucky, that I was a top girl. I worked damn hard, but there were three or four high earners and the rest took roughly half of what we did. The bottom girls were lucky to earn a quarter. I had known one girl go home with only £30 on more than one occasion. When you add up the hours, they would have earned more sitting behind a till at the local supermarket. Like any job, the money is good at the top but, unlike many, it can destroy you in more ways than one before you get there. I earned well, sure, but when I broke it down, it was only about twice what I earned in my previous normal job. But by then it wasn't just about the money any more. I was hooked on the whole set-up and keen to explore other money-making strands that allowed me lots of action.

I tallied up recently how many clients I had had sex with, and I realized I'd sat on a lot of cocks to pay the bills that year! I also realized how lucky I had been, as any of them could have been a complete nutter. I had decided that, going to London, I wanted to see half the men for at least twice the money if the stripping fell through and I was going to continue down the sex route.

I saw men of all races, mostly because I was petite. I was popular with the Chinese, Japanese, Arabs, and Indians. I entertained the odd American, Filipino, Russian, men from all over the UK...even saw an Eskimo once!

Have I serviced anyone famous? Sorry to spoil your fun but, even if I had, I would never shag and spill the beans...*no way*. Trust and discretion are all in this profession and my client confidentiality is like that shared by doctors and their patients.

I have sold my body to the masses, my soul to my lovers, so why not my story to the world?

What happened next? Well, that's another year...

Handy Hints for Hookers: Paid to get laid in a brothel 101

SEX TIPS

CONDOM USE

*M*y pet peeve about the industry has to be the urban myth of putting on a condom with just your mouth—"the suck-on method."

OK, let's get this straight. No matter what you have heard, seen in porn, or think you can do, you can in no way whatsoever put a rubber on safely just using your mouth. Every clinic I have ever been to will back me up. You might be able to just suck it on and get it to stay there, but now try and jump on board, ride it, and not have the damn thing come off at some point. It defeats the object, doesn't it?

I've heard it called all sorts, from the "tonsil technique" to "the hooker's way." Just because we call it "the suck-on method" doesn't mean we *just* suck it on. Got it? Good. There, I feel better getting that off my chest. Ignorance to me is never bliss. It just pisses me off.

I even had a client at one point who, when I had finished and was about to jump on top, said, "That was good, shame you have to put the rubber on now." He just wouldn't believe he was wearing one till he looked down, just because he hadn't felt me put it on. Just goes to show that some of the time it's all in a guy's head. A real man can wear a rubber with no problem—end of story. I pride myself on the fact I can put one on safely in under four seconds, what with all the practice, but it took ages to get the hang of it to start with. It saves a lot of time once you've learned how, because you're able to put it on when the man is soft—as soon as it's on you can suck it hard. Saves all the hand jobs to get it up, and then the droop by the time you've rolled the rubber down. Some guys would not know you had even put it on if you started sucking really hard and fast; you would have them up in no time. The skill is judging when to stop in time to sit on and ride!

The girls generally feel that rolling on a condom is a sure-fire way of letting a guy know you are new. Then it's like a red flag to take the piss and mess you around. They like to try it on with new girls because they know they can get away with it, or think they can, what with the "Well, such and such does this" and "The last girl let me rub my dick down her crack without the condom on. I won't go inside, I promise, ask any of the girls" and "What's-her-name does it without, you know—she's very popular" and "Sure it's safe to lick my balls—all the girls do it. If you're a good girl

I will give you a tip." Blah blah blah. Yes and those girls are very popular down the local clap clinic too, I want to add.

We tend not to roll it on like the packet says for our own safety and health reasons. If you catch something, you can't work, so you don't get paid. Ever heard "Watch the pennies and the pounds look after themselves"? More like, "Look after your health and it will look after your wallet" —simple as that. It's safer to do it our way because if you have been using your hand to touch/play with the guy to get the penis hard enough to roll the rubber on, then your hand could have picked up any bacteria on his cock, which would then be wiped on to the outside of the rubber as you roll it down. Then any bacteria that was on his cock would be on the outside of the rubber that is going into you. Not the most hygienic way to put one on: puts you at more risk with the amount of one-off clients we see. Sucking it on and unrolling it from the inside means that anything is left on the inside of the condom, not the outside, and the sucking creates a better vacuum, too.

In a room, with only thirty minutes of game play, you just don't have the time to wait around till he rises to the occasion without giving any help. If he's been on the booze a bit you really will need to give him a helping hand. Dutch courage will only help you post a French letter, not put one on. Also, it's quicker—three to five seconds—so the client doesn't have the time to go soft and waste time with all the Yo-Yo action. It also means he doesn't have time to start dicking around with the "I don't really like wearing a rubber" comment, because it 's on so quickly and if you start sucking it will distract him enough to direct his attention elsewhere. We don't tend to have the same guy to play with all the time, and action can be moved along a bit faster than among civilians, so we don't have the luxury of waiting till a guy is hard and ready before we touch him and then to fiddle with the faffy rolling-it-down condom thing. And in this day and age there is no way any lady in her right mind would trust a client to put it on. For a start, you never know what he may have done to the rubber or if he put it on correctly...also means you can suck one on a soft member to get it hard and change it when it is hard so you don't have to do dangerous OWO.

I am a rubber lover myself, as I have said. I can't stand to do it without: even when I have in the past on a tested boyfriend, I would still use a rubber. I do have friends who can't stand them, however, so I do understand.

It really is a show-how-to lesson rather than a read-how-to lesson. Most girls in agencies/houses or flats learn it from the other girls. I will try to explain, but I am warning you now that I take no responsibility if the rubber pings off into your mouth and you nearly choke or take someone's eye out trying it. I also take no responsibility should a lady acciden-tally ping the rubber. It is normally sneaky payback for a client dicking about. "I am soo sorry!" we say with big-eyed concern. I laugh myself silly when a client says he doesn't like it put on like that because girls can twang the rubber. You just know why girls have being doing that and what to expect from him next if it has happened to him more than once with different girls—unless all he picks are new girls, who are experimenting on him, that is; more likely he is a handful in the bedroom, and not a good one either.

How to do it

Take the rubber out of the packet by the rim only between thumb and index finger. You will be able to tell the inside as the teat is on the other side. Hold it teat up by the rim and put three middle fingers of each hand inside. Hold it by the rim now with both thumbs on the outside rim, the three fingers of each hand still inside. Pull your hands apart so the condom stretches to accommodate.

OK so far? Tricky bit coming up...

While still holding the rubber in two hands, suck the teat on to the head of the cock. When sucked on the head, take your thumbs away and start to roll it down from the inside with your fingers still inside.

Bit tricky to explain this bit: rolling it down from the inside just needs a hell of a lot of practice. You need to keep it stretched apart and roll it down by using all the inside fingers in a caterpillar motion, pushing fingers up and pulling down as you suck down at the same time.

If he's hard, carry on till unrolled and gently slide fingers out until you are holding the rubber with thumbs and index fingers. Let go at the end as you continue to suck...If he's soft, hold the rubber stretched open as you suck down and hold with both hands at the base, so it is not restrictive to his blood flow, and continue the blow-job till he's hard...Take off the rubber with a tissue and put on a fresh one (if you use a flavoured one, it's a great excuse to change it).

BLOW-JOBS

Not really sure how to explain giving head. It just came naturally to me. Overwhelming the sense of power, the power I feel from sucking a cock, knowing he has his life in my mouth—one hard BITE and it could all be over. Gives me a thrill it gives such pleasure.

I start a blow-job by sucking down on to a rubbered dick, pressing my tongue up against the shaft. Keeping the suction, I begin slowly to move up and down the shaft, then speed up. Putting my hand around the base of the cock stops me going too far and gagging if my head is suddenly pushed down on an excited member by its enthusiastic owner. Looking up into the man's eyes as he is watching you giving head must be so horny—I always get a groan when I do that.

Girls, if you are going to follow this advice, be careful: not all men are the same. Some are very sensitive boys and need you to go slow with the sucking. Some don't like a strong suck at all and, in very rare cases, they can find it extremely painful.

Hot and cold blow-jobs

Ice cubes or iced water and hot tea are the main ingredients in a hot and cold blow-job (it took me a week not to giggle whenever I picked up a tea cup after my first time), although hot chocolate makes a great substitute, and a stickier option is ice cream and hot fudge sauce, so I'm told.

It's extremely messy, and I had to put towels down first to catch the liquid, but the result is much appreciated by the gentleman concerned. I didn't offer this service unless asked; as you can imagine, it's a big hassle to clean up. I don't recommend it unless he wants sex and she has a craving for chocolate!

Geminis and Lesbian Shows

If you're someone who really can't face a face full of fanny, try putting your hand over the other girl's muff and lick your fingers instead. Flicking your hair over so it hides what you are doing can help too. If you have short hair, it's easier to put a hand under her rump, cup your hand over her, and then do it as, with your head on top, the view is a bit restricted. If you are going to use a dildo, doggie for the recipient is going to be best and, for goodness' sake, use a soft one and go slow, as it's more show for him than anything.

Watersports

Not a chance of getting a slack fanny with this manoeuvre. Muscles down below, like any other muscle, get stronger with use. I'm talking of the one set of particular muscles you can feel if you squeeze to stop in the middle of peeing. Those pelvic-floor muscles are extremely handy if you want to prolong a golden shower. Watersports is not something that every girl will feel comfortable doing, but hey—if a guy gets turned on by being pissed on, I don't mind obliging. As long as he doesn't want to piss on me, that's fine.

Guzzling at least two pints of water before going down to see a regular you know likes this really helps. You can do it in the shower, or a bath is even better. If you're doing it on a bed it's best to put lots of towels down first. Laying the client down in a bath of warm water is always a good option, as you can shower him from head to foot by standing above or squatting over the bath. Some like to gargle with it if you pee over their face. If they request this, just watch out they don't spit it back, as it gets messy. For the majority, though, it's a passing fantasy and the client will like to wank off as you piss on their cock.

TALKING DIRTY

This is a request I personally hate. It's hard to do when you have your mind on all sorts of other things. Am I running out of time? Is the receptionist going to knock on the door any minute? Can I get into a position to feel if the condom is still there? What's the daft bugger doing with that hand now? If I fake an "I am coming" squeal, will he stop poking me so damn hard? He better come soon!

It's quite easy for your mind to draw a blank and if he is good at what he's doing and he asks in the middle of things, it can break your concentration. It can make you freeze and bring you down to earth in a moment. Clients don't usually think to ask you beforehand, for some reason—not that most of them have the time or the nerve.

What do you say? I found out that having watched a bit of porno helps a lot, and magazines are a good one to get dirty lines from, too. Porno in the room is a whole different matter and might just give them the wrong idea and they might start messing you around. Looking at that stuff you realize why men come out with some of the stupid lines and daft requests they do: they get most of it from porno.

It took months of working to feel easy about talking dirty and not to giggle, feeling embarrassed, at the "Come on, then, boy, fuck me harder!" "Faster," and all the other lines that come to mind. It helps saying a few lines over and over again out loud to yourself in the mirror—at least till you can stop giggling. The novelty will wear off and you will stop feeling embarrassed, but it might take longer to master than anything else.

DOMINATION

Credit to the Dommes of this world, doing the worst "head-screw" job of all time. Ladies, I salute you! It takes a strong person to deal with all the crap that goes with it; it leaves you feeling drained, mentally exhausted—much more than straight sex ever can.

You think it's easy? Why does everyone think it's easy?

Think again, it's not. It does not just mean shouting at a guy and kicking him, beating him stupid, and him paying you for the privilege to whip him/it. Domination is never that easy. Every client is different—they like different things, have different fetishes—and if you get it wrong or don't know what you're doing, all hell can break loose. Not all submissives are masochists, i.e., not all of them like pain, though, saying that, if you enjoy anal, then you are definitely a sub, no question. There are different types of pain, after all. Some subs just like to be teased, some like to be tied up and deprived, and some just like watersports.

The list is endless. Even in the foot-fetishism kingdom not all guys like to suck toes. For example, some just get off on the feel of nylon, some like their foot Miss to wear tights they can rub up against, some like bare legs and high heels or to be trampled on. My point is that, for a Domme, it's a wide-reaching fetish net and it's not all about "whipping some guy." Creativity, imagination, sheer force of will, the ability to control a situation, adaptability, and experience help someone become a Domme. It's not something you can just learn off the bat in an A–Z book of domination. When you get into it, it's not nearly as simple as it all looks. It is all well and good if you can find a book, but experience counts a great deal over anything you can read. You either cope or you don't. If you're the slightest bit squeamish, I suggest you don't even poke S&M with a barge pole (think I will definitely leave domming till I am older and wiser).

HEALTH TIPS

RUBBER CARE

Don't let a client get you in a position where you can't reach for a rubber. A condom tucked in the top of stocking hold-ups is a handy place. Always take at least five rubbers with you. If you only take one and it splits while going on (very rare) or he's up and down like a Yo-Yo needing a new one, you're screwed...or not, as the case may be. And for goodness' sake, with condoms, don't go putting one on over the other, thinking two is safer than one; the friction between the two can split them both.

RIGHT-HAND/LEFT-HAND USE

The universal consensus is that you use your watch hand (usually your left) to touch yourself, and your other hand (the right) to touch the client. It is cleaner that way and easy to remember. If you use the same hand all the time, you don't forget. It's difficult enough trying to keep an eye on where the client's hands have been and are going as it is.

CUP CARE

Swirl cups out with boiling water before making a drink to make sure they are clean. In a workplace used by many people, not everyone may have the same standards of hygiene as you. Your body is literally your livelihood. If you catch something, you will have to take time off till you are clear or you might have to stop work full stop! A devastating thought. Anything that cuts down even the smallest risks to your health is good. If you can't work, what a waste of sexual opportunities and earning potential it is. Looking after yourself is common sense; it means you have the capacity to earn more.

SMELLIES

Do not wear perfume unless you know the client very well, as a wife might smell it on her husband, which will get him into trouble and he might not come back to see you again, losing you potential custom. Use men's deodorant instead if you have to—it is less suspicious if the smell rubs off.

TOYS

Wash your vibrators in boiling water and put a condom on them straight after use to keep them clean when they are in your drawer or bag. I always use a new rubber each time I use one to keep bacteria at bay and the vibrator ready for action.

OWO

Oral WithOut a condom. The choice is totally up to the house where the girl works, but most houses are smart enough to know the kind of damage unprotected services can do to its girls and clientele. If one girl goes down with something nasty, it will not earn the house money if she has to stop working or quit because of it. And if it hits one girl it could spread like wildfire throughout the other workers in the house. Also, you end up with the high-roller clients, who are normally the more intelligent educated guys (that's how they became high-rollers in the first place) going elsewhere. They are not stupid and normally have their health in mind as well as wanting to have fun. They will take their money/business to better and cleaner houses that do have health-educated girls or stricter house rules. Just because a house offers all sorts of services, it doesn't necessarily mean it will have a higher turnover.

HOUSE AND GENERAL ETIQUETTE

Sex tips can get you only so far in the game. You need to pay attention to all sides of a complex situation: clients, the girls, and the people you work for.

There are a few things you just don't ask other girls in a house unless you really want to dig a hole for yourself. Along with a few unwritten rules, I learned some the hard way and observed some in the messy aftermath.

- "The golden rule": always get your money upfront no matter what anyone says at the time. Don't even get as far as naked till you're paid and have checked the money. You're not a stripper—you're not working for tips (no offence to dancers—I have been there too—but it's not the same type of work).

- Never ask another girl how much she has earned or how many clients she has seen. It's just plain rude, the same as it is in any business.

- Don't ask to borrow money from another girl. She has risked her life with every client she sees for that cash. Even if you plan to give it back the next day, the damage is done. Your credibility has gone to hell in a handbag, honey.

- Never brag about how many clients you have seen or how much you got in tips, unless you want nasty "she does extras" rumours. Jealous girls don't pull punches if they can interrupt your business and direct it to themselves.

- Don't expect another girl to do something you would not do yourself. Same goes for never working for someone who wouldn't do or hasn't done what you will do. You will not have their respect and they will take the piss out of you in the end.

- Outside the house most girls will pass each other by without a second glance. It's not that they don't like you, it's more an issue of mutual respect. They don't know who is with you or who's watching and do not want to put you in a situation that will arouse any questions. The same goes, without saying, for clients.

- Bad-mouthing other girls behind their backs is just plain bad karma. Girls get enough verbal from clients as it is: if you can't say anything nice, don't say anything at all. It just belittles you.

- In the house, no matter where you are, always call a girl by her working name. You never know who's listening.

- Never discuss a client with another girl if he is in the next room as he might be able to hear you. Includes waiting to say hello, too. Walls can be thin in a bordello, don't you know?

- If a guy is in with his friends and they are in the next room, it always helps to make some extra effort and noise. He will get a pat on the back from his mates later and it will do his morale a lot of good, so he is more likely to come back and see you. Also, his friends will be intrigued to know what was going on and come back to see you too. Oh, best to warn the receptionist that you might be extra noisy when going to the room, as you don't want her bursting in thinking you are in trouble and screaming for help. It can put a guy off his stroke if the door flies open!

- Don't be too pissed off if you are new and hardly any girls talk to you. It's probably not because they don't like you personally, it's just that at least two out of three girls (in my experience) will leave the house after a few shifts if it is not for them. Most of the long-standing girls will see if you can stick it for a bit and gain their respect before even talking to you. It's hard to keep on making friends with everyone all the time and then not see them again. Failing that, though, if you are stunning and they think you will take their custom, they will try to make you feel as uncomfortable as possible to get you to leave.

- Don't ask other girls too many personal questions, especially if you are new. If you have just arrived, have not seen any clients, and are asking every question under the sun, everyone is going to think you are a copper, someone from the council, or, more likely, a journalist. You are going to be given the cold shoulder faster than you can put a rubber on.

TO STAY AHEAD OF THE GAME IN-HOUSE

- Keep your gob shut. Remember that a closed mouth gathers no foot. If your mouth is open all the time gabbing, then you're not learning anything that can help you.

- The owner/manager is not your friend. No matter how nice they are, they are in the same business as you—making money—but they are using you to make it, so of course they are going to be nice, to keep on your good side so you stay working for them. Just bear that in mind.

- You gain a damn good shit-detector pretty fast. Trust your instincts and 98 percent of the time you will be right. If you don't like a situation or the way it is turning, make your excuses and get out. Remember: if it sounds too good to be true, it is.

- If you're not happy or comfortable doing something, don't do it, no matter what. There are always other houses, other ways to make money, no matter how desperate you are. Compromising your values will only make you feel crappy and bring you down, and that in turn makes you vulnerable and at risk, giving out the signal for people to treat you like shit. It won't be profitable looking like a wet weekend, as clients won't pick you and the owners will take advantage and try and squeeze more money out of you, at your expense and the expense of your health.

- Stick to your boundaries. At the end of the day, you are the only one who has your best interests at heart. Sad but true.

- Redirection: if a guy is trying to get you to do something you don't do or don't want to do, or you can see it coming, try to redirect rather than saying no directly. It can work much better to say, for example, "That does not really do anything for me, but I would love it if you—" (even if he was asking for his benefit). Just keep talking enthusiastically to keep things moving on; most of the time it works like a charm. Raising your voice or sometimes just saying "no" can aggravate the situation, which doesn't help at all if they are a bit pissed or generally being an arsehole. It can keep a client from getting annoyed and turning on you in frustration. That doesn't mean you shouldn't say a direct "no" if he takes the condom off or is being violent, though. If it comes to that, the situation has gone too far and it's not your fault. You should be looking for the exit, an excuse to leave, or be calling for help.

- The "headfuck": it is going to happen. No matter how much you have read or think you know before you start, or even how stable you think you are, the paranoia will screw with your head at some point. In some cases, it has been known to happen months later. Just remember: you're not alone, so don't panic. There is no right way to deal with it: as far as I know every girl deals with it differently. You deal with it or you leave the job, plain and simple.

- Never ever trust a client. You might have known him for ages, he might be really nice or give you the best orgasm of your life but most will push you to your boundaries to get as much out of you as they can. At the end of the day, he's still a client and it's best it stays that way. It sounds harsh and I do love men, honest—don't get me wrong—but the client/working girl relationship does not work well for very long if the client stops paying.

- The house has eyes and ears everywhere. If you're stupid enough to think you're not going to get caught by flouting one of the house rules, you better pack your bag now, honey, because you're on your way out soon.

- Don't dramatically change your looks, for example, extra tattoos, facial piercings, brightly colouring your hair, or shaving it off (even if it's your preference), as this can downgrade your earning potential. Hold off on your personal desires if you don't want it to hit your pocket. I am still amazed at the amount of girls who didn't realize that it would have a knock-on effect on their earning potential till after they'd done it.

BUSINESS FOOTNOTE

Non-communicative women who let guys get away with bad sex do men no favours. The woman in question is bound to walk away and leave the guy still thinking he's a stud when he's not, and then he passes his bad habits on to other conquests, who also then make noises of loud content to get it over with quickly. Then they leave the guy soon after without saying anything, just "It's not you, it's me," or some other excuse rather than telling him, for example, that he kisses like a troll or has poked her so hard she has bruises on her thighs well into the next week.

On the other hand, it does us working girls a good turn. We see a lot of these type of guys in a house. They come in with poor technique and, quite frankly, it's bad business to fix them and set them straight. Who has time anyway, in a thirty-minute slot? (Married men are a whole different ball game; after one or two kids the wife's libido normally disappears, in most cases along with her figure, so married men might love their wives but think they shouldn't bother them with their basic needs, so they go elsewhere.) Men with bad technique are a hassle to deal with, sure, but if they get good and know what to do, they don't have to come back, do they? They get all confident and girlfriends no longer leave them.

Correcting bad technique is bad for business, the bosses always said. "It would be a bit like taking your car to the garage and, rather than the mechanic just repairing it, teaching you how to so you wouldn't need to go back or pay them again." It's bad for the brothel's pocket in the long run. We can practise safe sex in a brothel, but it doesn't mean we have to teach good sex, now does it? People have urges—it's inbuilt human nature—but ignorant and sexually uneducated people make the worst lovers. The more you know, the better the sex.

Conclusion: Abstinence is not safer sex! Knowledge is.